From Your Friends At **The Mailbox**

APRIL

A MONTH OF IDEAS AT YOUR FINGERTIPS!

GRADES 1–3

D1539741

WRITTEN BY
Resa Audet, Ada Hamrick, Alma Hoffman,
Nicole Iacovazzi, Stacie Stone, Kathy Wolf

EDITED BY
Lynn Bemer Coble, Jennifer Rudisill,
Gina Sutphin, Kathy Wolf

ILLUSTRATED BY
Jennifer Tipton Bennett
Cathy Spangler Bruce
Teresa Davidson
Barry Slate
Donna K. Teal

COVER ART BY
Jennifer Tipton Bennett

www.themailbox.com

Manufactured in the United States
10 9 8 7 6 5

TABLE OF CONTENTS

April Calendar

Keep America Beautiful Month

The focus for April is on beautifying and caring for the world around us. This month we celebrate Earth Day, Arbor Day, and Keep America Beautiful Month, which began as a single-day celebration in 1971. Local affiliates of Keep America Beautiful, Inc., a national, nonprofit organization, will plan all sorts of activities to clean up the environment—from litter pickups to recycling, from building parks to making posters with environmental messages. For more information, you can write to Keep America Beautiful, Inc., 9 West Broad Street, Stamford, CT 06902. Consider conducting a class project for the month of April to help beautify your school grounds!

Mathematics Education Month

April is the month to think about math! We all use math every day, whether going to the grocery store, setting the alarm clock, or serving up a pizza. Take time this month to focus on the importance of math in everyday life and in careers such as medicine and engineering. Read some great literature links, such as *Each Orange Had Eight Slices* by Paul Giganti, Jr. (Greenwillow Books, 1992) or *Bunches And Bunches Of Bunnies* by Louise Mathews (Scholastic Inc., 1978). Then ask students to make up a "math story" of their own.

National Library Month

What a great month to celebrate libraries! International Children's Book Day falls on April 2 (see below), April 9 is the anniversary of the first free public library opening in the United States (in 1833), and April 24 is the anniversary of the establishment of the Library of Congress (in 1800). Be sure to take your students to visit the school or public library during the month of April. Read *I Took My Frog To The Library* by Eric Kimmel (Puffin Books, 1990); then discuss appropriate library behavior.

1—April Fools' Day

The first day of April kicks off National Humor Month with a day of pranks and trickery! No one is sure how it began, but April Fools' Day has been celebrated for centuries. Read *It's April Fools' Day* by Steven Kroll (Scholastic Inc., 1990); then tell students that laughter is good for their health as well as their attitude. Let students write their favorite jokes and illustrate them to share with classmates.

2—International Children's Book Day

This day celebrates children's literature and commemorates the birthday of Hans Christian Andersen, author of more than 150 fairy tales. (See pages 26–30 for activities linked to Andersen's books.) Celebrate literacy today by inviting guest readers (parents, the principal, local sports stars, or TV personalities) to read their favorite stories to your class. Have students make bookmarks with drawings of their favorite story characters.

3—Inauguration Of The Pony Express

The first rider in the Pony Express left St. Joseph, Missouri, on this date in 1860, traveling west to Sacramento, California. Another rider left from Sacramento on April 4, heading east. It cost $5 an ounce to deliver a letter, and delivery took up to ten days. The riders each rode 75 to 100 miles, and there were 190 way stations along the route. The Pony Express ran for less than two years, before being replaced by transcontinental railroads.

(Turn the page for more...)

Ask students if they would have liked to hold this postal delivery job. Then discuss the changes in mail delivery since the time of the Pony Express. For more information, read *The Post Office Book: Mail And How It Moves* by Gail Gibbons (HarperCollins Children's Books, 1986).

7—World Health Day

This day was established in 1948 by WHO, the World Health Organization. Its objective is to remind people about good health habits. Each year the event is based on a different theme, such as "Heartbeat—The Rhythm Of Health" or "Oral Health For A Healthy Life." Invite your students to participate in World Health Day by creating posters promoting good health habits, such as eating right, exercising, or brushing teeth regularly. Display the posters around your classroom or school.

12—Anniversary Of The First Space Shuttle Launch

The first space shuttle, *Columbia*, was launched on this day in 1981. This was the first manned spaceflight since *Apollo-Soyuz* in 1976. Two astronauts orbited the earth 36 times before landing on April 14.

Share *The Magic School Bus Lost In The Solar System* by Joanna Cole (Scholastic Inc., 1990). Ask students to write about what they'd like to see if they traveled through space in a space shuttle.

19—Beginning Of The American Revolution

On this date in 1775, the American Revolution began with the battles at Lexington and Concord, Massachusetts. The Battle of Concord was the first decisive victory for American colonists who caused British forces to retreat to Boston. Ralph Waldo Emerson coined the famous phrase "the shot heard round the world" in reference to this battle. Have students locate Concord and Boston on a map and use the map key to determine how far British forces had to retreat.

22—Earth Day

Since 1970, a day in April has been set aside to encourage people to protect and preserve the earth and our natural resources. Read *For The Love Of Our Earth* by P. K. Hallinan (Ideals Children's Books, 1992) and try some of the Earth Day activities on pages 31–40.

30—Anniversary Of Regular Television Broadcasting

On this date in 1939, NBC broadcast a show about the opening of the World's Fair in New York. But because of World War II and the Korean War (which meant a shortage of necessary materials for continuing research and building TV sets), television didn't become popular until the 1950s.

Ask students to list all the shows they watch on a regular basis, then calculate the number of hours they spend watching TV each day. Create a graph to show the results. Then read *The Berenstain Bears And Too Much TV* by Stan and Jan Berenstain (Random House Books For Young Readers, 1984).

National Arbor Day

Arbor Day is a day for honoring trees! It is held on varying dates in different states, but most states observe it on the last Friday in April. Read *A Tree Is Nice* by Janice M. Udry (HarperCollins Children's Books, 1987) and discuss the many benefits of trees. Then try some of the activities on pages 41–50.

CLASSROOM TIMES

Teacher:_____ Date:_____

APRIL

Events

Reminders

Superstars

Special Thanks

Help Wanted

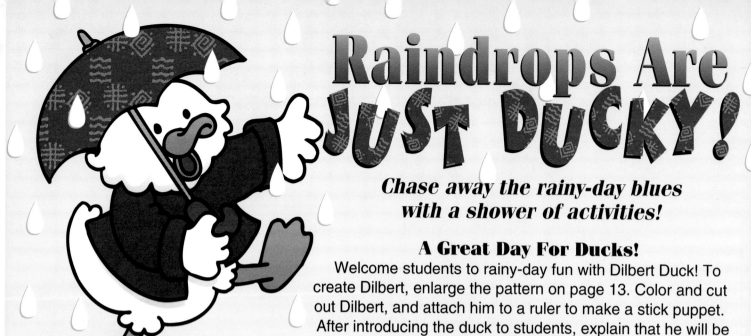

Raindrops Are JUST DUCKY!

Chase away the rainy-day blues with a shower of activities!

A Great Day For Ducks!

Welcome students to rainy-day fun with Dilbert Duck! To create Dilbert, enlarge the pattern on page 13. Color and cut out Dilbert, and attach him to a ruler to make a stick puppet. After introducing the duck to students, explain that he will be helping them learn about rain. Ask students if they, like Dilbert, think rain is just ducky! Challenge students to tell why rain is helpful to humans— and ducks! List all the students' responses on the board. Then provide each student with a raindrop cutout. Instruct students to write on their cutouts the ways that rain is helpful to all living things. When they finish, add the cutouts to the bulletin board described below.

Just Ducky!

Decorate your bulletin board with these delightful ducks! Cover your board with light blue or navy blue background paper. Provide each student with a copy of the duck patterns on page 14, glue, scissors, yellow and black construction paper, yellow and orange crayons, two wiggly eyes, wallpaper scraps and an umbrella pattern. Instruct each student to color the duck's body yellow, and its feet and bill orange. Cut out all the pieces; then glue the bill and the feet to the body. To make the duck's wings, each student traces her hands on yellow construction paper and cuts them out. Glue the wings to the back of the duck's body. To complete the duck, glue on two wiggly eyes.

Next have students trace and cut umbrellas from wallpaper scraps. Cut handles from black construction paper and attach them to the bottoms of the umbrellas. Glue each umbrella to a duck's wing as shown. Mount the ducks on the bulletin board along with the raindrop cutouts and the title "Rain Is Just Ducky!"

RAIN IS JUST DUCKY!

Drip, Drop, Don't Stop...Reading, That Is!

Encourage students to read different books from literature genres with the help of this bulletin board. Begin by covering your bulletin board with blue background paper. Enlarge and color the cat-and-dog pattern on page 13, and mount it on the board. Then trace and cut out several large umbrellas from different colors of construction paper. Program each umbrella with a different literature genre. Construct handles from construction paper and attach them to the umbrellas. Mount the umbrellas on the bulletin board and add the title "It's Raining Books!" As each student finishes reading a book, he writes a summary on a raindrop cutout. Mount the cutouts under the appropriate umbrellas.

Like Water Off A Duck's Back

Ask students to speculate why Dilbert doesn't get soaking wet when he's in the water. Then explain that a duck has a gland located at the base of its tail feathers that secretes an oil. This oil covers the duck's feathers so that water is *repelled*.

Determine whether or not certain objects will *absorb* water or *repel* water like a duck's feathers. Divide students into small groups and provide each group with a container of water, an eyedropper, and various waterproof and nonwaterproof items such as waxed paper, a Styrofoam® cup, and a tissue. Have groups place items on their workspaces one at a time. Instruct each group to use the eyedropper to put drops of water on each item. Have students observe whether or not the water beads up and rolls off the object (is repelled) or is absorbed. Encourage each student to record his findings on a chart similar to the one shown. Conclude the lesson by discussing items that are *waterproof* and those that aren't.

Name **Dilbert Duck**

Object	Absorbs (Water soaks in.)	Repels (Water beads up.)
waxed paper		✓
Styrofoam® cup		✓
tissue	✓	

Raindrops Keep Falling On My Head!

Pique students' interest in the *water cycle* when you explain that the water on earth today is the same water that was on earth millions of years ago. In fact, students could be drinking the same water that dinosaurs once drank!

Help students better understand the natural phenomena of the water cycle by sharing the story *Water's Way* by Lisa Westberg Peters (Scholastic Inc., 1991). Referring to the photos in the story, discuss the words *evaporation, condensation,* and *precipitation.* List them on the board and briefly explain each one. Then provide students with copies of the water cycle reproducible on page 15. Instruct students to cut out the words, glue them in to the appropriate boxes and draw arrows. Then engage students in the three experiments that follow to help them better understand the water cycle.

Evaluating Evaporation

Investigate *evaporation!* Explain that evaporation occurs when the heat of the sun causes water to turn into tiny droplets—called *water vapor*—that rise into the air. Then have each student pick a partner, and provide each pair with two, four-ounce clear plastic cups; masking tape; a small piece of foil; and two sheets of paper. Instruct student pairs to fill both cups half full of water. Have students use pieces of masking tape to mark the water levels on the outsides of the cups. Instruct students to use the foil to cover *one* cup. Set all of the cups in the sun. Next instruct students to fold their papers in fourths and then unfold them to create four boxes. Have each student draw and label pictures of the cups as they appear on Day 1 of the experiment in the top two boxes.

Leave the cups in the sun for four days. Then have students work with their partners to compare the water levels on Day 4 of the experiment to the water levels on Day 1 of the experiment (on their pictures). Encourage students to hypothesize why the water level in one cup is lower than the water level in the other cup. Then instruct students to draw and label pictures of the cups as they appear on Day 4 of the experiment in the bottom two boxes on their papers. Conclude the lesson with a discussion of students' observations. Guide students to the discoveries that the water in the uncovered cup evaporated and the foil covering the other cup prevented the water from evaporating.

Condensation Is Cool!

Get a close-up look at *condensation!* Explain that water vapor does not always stay in the air. When water vapor cools, it changes from an invisible gas to droplets of water—this is called *condensation*.

Expand your discussion on condensation with this experiment. Divide students into pairs and provide each pair with two glasses, three ice cubes, and two sheets of paper. Instruct students to fill one of their glasses with warm water and the other with cold water. Have students place their ice cubes into the glass of cold water. Set the glasses aside for a few minutes.

While students are waiting, have them divide their papers into sections by folding them in fourths, and then unfolding them. Instruct students to draw and label pictures of the glasses as they initially appeared in the top two boxes. After a few minutes, have students observe their glasses. In the bottom two boxes on their papers, students draw and label pictures of the glasses as they now appear.

Encourage each student pair to make a hypothesis about why water droplets appeared on the outside of the cold glass but not on the warm glass. Guide students to the discovery that condensation occurred when the water vapor in the air touched the cold glass and was cooled. This caused the water vapor to turn into tiny water droplets. When the water vapor in the air touched the warm glass, it was not cooled so it did not condense. Students will agree that condensation is cool!

Pondering Precipitation

Demonstrate how *precipitation* occurs with a little help from a hot plate, a tray of ice cubes, two oven mitts, and a teakettle full of water. But first explain that as water vapor cools and condenses, it turns into tiny water droplets that form *clouds*. As each droplet falls through a cloud, it combines with many other droplets, resulting in precipitation. Precipitation is any moisture that falls from clouds—*rain, snow, hail,* or *sleet*.

To begin the experiment, place the teakettle on the hot plate. When steam begins to escape from the teakettle, use oven mitts to hold a tray of ice cubes about five inches above the steam. Explain that as water from the kettle evaporates, it collects where the air is cool. When several water droplets combine beneath the ice-cube tray, a raindrop is formed and it falls downward. Distribute sheets of white paper to students and have the papers fold them in half. Instruct students to draw and label pictures showing the beginning and the end of the experiment.

Complete The Cycle

At the conclusion of your lessons, bind each student's experiment picture sheets between student-made covers to create individual booklets. Title the booklets "Our Wonderful Water Cycle" and allow students to take them home.

A Day In The Life Of A Raindrop

Assess students' knowledge of the water cycle. Divide students into groups and encourage each group to write a short play about a raindrop and its travels through the water cycle. Challenge each group to name its raindrop; then ask students to think about the following questions: "Where would your raindrop start its journey? What would happen to the raindrop after it had evaporated? Condensed? Fallen as precipitation?" After groups have written their scripts, allow them to make simple props, masks, and backdrops in order to present their plays to classmates.

Rain Gauge

Make a gauge to help students measure rainfall at school. To complete this project, you will need an empty two-liter plastic bottle, a funnel, a ruler, a permanent marker, a wooden stake or dowel, and two large rubber bands. Use the ruler and marker to denote a desired scale on the side of the bottle. Drive the stake into level ground in an open area and set the bottle beside it. Secure the bottle to the stake with the rubber bands. Place the funnel inside the bottle as shown. Each day allow a pair of students to take a reading of the amount of rainfall collected and record it on a classroom calendar. Remind students that each time a measurement is recorded, the rainwater should be poured out and the bottle secured to the stake again. At the end of a predetermined amount of time, determine as a class how much rain has fallen or how many days were without rain.

Rainfall Comparisons

Engage students in an activity that compares life in the desert to life in the rain forest. Explain that rain forests are areas where *at least* 100 inches of rainfall in any given year. Desert areas, on the other hand, receive only trace amounts of rainfall.

Locate rain forest areas and desert areas on a world map. Remind students that either too little or too much rain can pose problems if plants, animals, and humans have not adapted to the situation. Then share the stories *Life In The Deserts* by Lucy Baker (Scholastic Inc., 1992) and *At Home In The Rain Forest* by Diane Willow (Charlesbridge Publishing, 1991). The stories describe plants and animals that make their homes in these areas. Enlist students' help in creating a chart of similarities and differences among plants and animals in these regions.

We are raindrops falling to the ocean.

Pitter-Patter—It's Poetry!

Brighten up a gloomy day by creating some rainy-day poetry! Set the mood for this activity by sharing weather-related poetry such as *Rainy Day: Stories And Poems* by Caroline F. Bauer (Lipp Junior Books, 1986). Then turn off the lights, turn on a nature recording of a rainstorm, and let students' imaginations run wild! After a predetermined amount of time, turn off the music and distribute a large raindrop cutout to each student. Tell students that they will be writing a rainy-day poem using four lines. Explain that the first line contains two words, the second line: four, the third line: six, and the fourth line: eight. After children have finished their poems and have had a chance to share their work, punch a hole at the top of each cutout and then bind all the cutouts together with a ring. Title the class collection "Pitter-Patter Poetry."

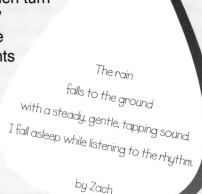

The rain
falls to the ground
with a steady, gentle, tapping sound.
I fall asleep while listening to the rhythm.

by Zach

Cloudy With A Chance Of Meatballs

You've heard of it raining cats and dogs? Well, this activity creates some even stranger weather phenomena. Share the story *Cloudy With A Chance Of Meatballs* by Judi Barrett (Atheneum Children's Book, 1978). This story describes some pretty un-usual forms of rain! Challenge students to brainstorm and illustrate other types of ridicu-lous rain. Then supply students with a copy of a sheet titled "The [name of your town] Daily News." Ask students to pretend that they are news reporters covering the strange, weather-related events that are occurring in town. When students have finished writing their fast-breaking news, have them share their stories with classmates. Bind the work into a book titled "Preposterous Precipitation."

Under The Weather

Create this learning center to practice basic math facts and num-ber order. Trace and cut out six umbrellas from colored construction paper, and glue to a file folder. Draw in umbrella handles with a black marker, and then program each of the umbrellas with a range of num-bers as shown. Trace and cut out 30 raindrops from white construction paper. Program the cutouts with math problems and code the backs for self-checking.

To play, place the cutouts in a pile faceup. A student picks a raindrop, solves the problem, and flips the card over to see if he answered correctly. He then places the rain-drop under the umbrella that shows the range of numbers in which the answer falls.

Use with "Drip, Drop, Don't Stop…Reading That Is!" on page 7.

13

Patterns
Use with "Just Ducky!" on page 6.

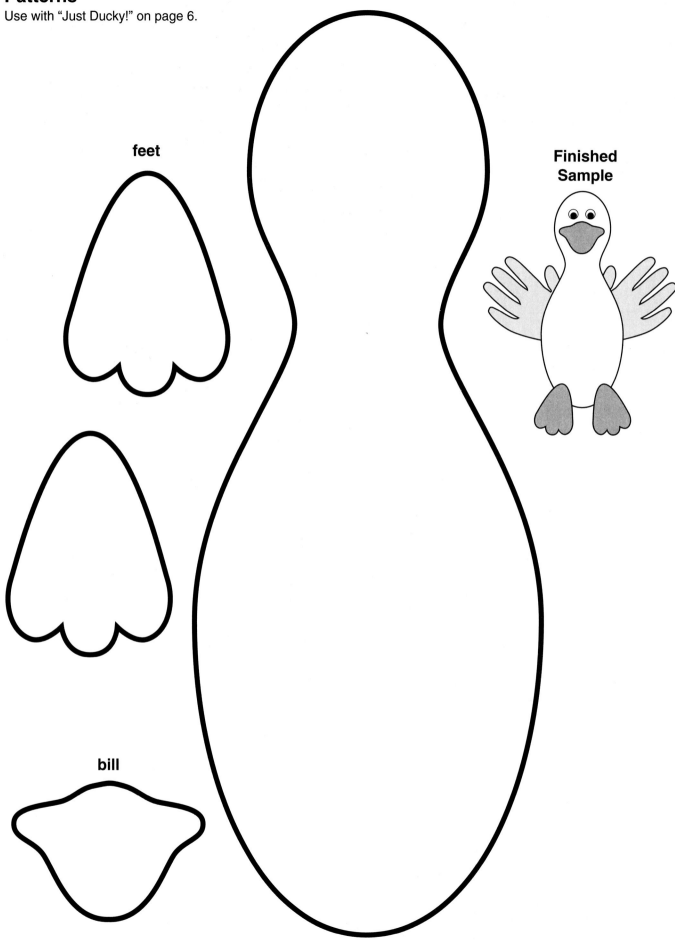

feet

bill

Finished Sample

Our Wonderful Water Cycle

Cut and paste the words in the correct boxes.
Draw arrows to show the water cycle.

| Precipitation | Condensation | Evaporation |

Note To The Teacher: Use this reproducible with "Raindrops Keep Falling On My Head!" on page 8.

The Rainbow

Help students understand how a rainbow paints the sky with its color!

Pretty Prism Projects

Explain to students that a rainbow occurs when sunlight passes through rain droplets. Each rain droplet acts like a tiny mirror—it reflects the light rays that go into the drop. This creates color because, although the sun's light looks white, it's actually a mixture of all colors. So, as the light enters and leaves the raindrops, its colors are bent—forming a rainbow.

Let students make their own indoor rainbows that would make every Pollyanna proud! Pick a sunny day and provide students with prisms. Have students hold their prisms up to a window and watch as rainbows dance around the room!

Mirror Rainbows

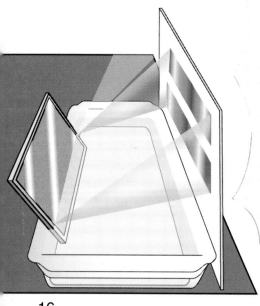

Try your hand at making indoor rainbows! Divide children into pairs. Provide each student pair with a shallow glass baking dish, a mirror, a flashlight, and a piece of heavy white paper. Have students in each pair fill their dish half full of water. Instruct them to rest their mirror at a 45-degree angle against the side of the dish (use pieces of clay to hold the mirror in place, if needed). Have students hold their paper at the side of the dish opposite their mirror. Next have students in each pair shine their flashlight on the section of the mirror that is underwater. Experiment with the position of the flashlight until a small rainbow is reflected onto the paper. Conclude the lesson by discussing students' observations.

Connection

Write Me A Rainbow

Nurture students' creative side with this writing activity. Duplicate the rainbow writing sheet found on page 21 and distribute to students. Obtain an overhead projector and place a glass pie plate that has been partially filled with water on the screen. Pour 1/4 cup of cooking oil into the dish; then add a few drops of red food coloring. The food coloring will stay on top of the oil, resulting in an interesting design. While this is happening, students should fill in the red band on their sheets, writing about how red makes them feel, or what red reminds them of. Then add a touch of yellow food coloring, creating an orange display, and have students fill in this band on their sheets. Repeat this procedure (changing oil and water as necessary) until the rainbows are completed. Encourage students to share their writing rainbows with classmates.

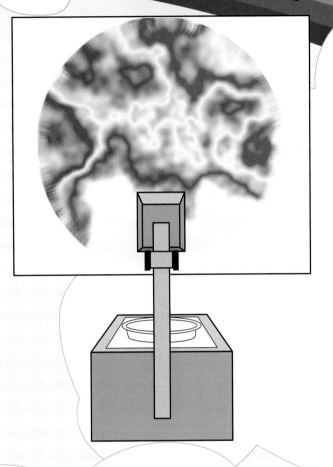

Somewhere Over The Rainbow

Share what people long ago believed to be true about rainbows. Explain that years ago, rainbows were misunderstood. People found them beautiful, magical, and frightening! Stories that were made up, over time, were believed. One story said that a rainbow was a bridge between heaven and earth; others said that a rainbow was a giant snake slithering across the sky; still others said that a pot of gold could be found at the end of a rainbow!

Then have students tell what rainbows remind them of—maybe they are slides for fairies, or multilane highways for leprechauns! Then encourage students to write their own stories about rainbows. Allow students to illustrate and share their stories. Then bind them into a classroom book titled "Somewhere Over The Rainbow."

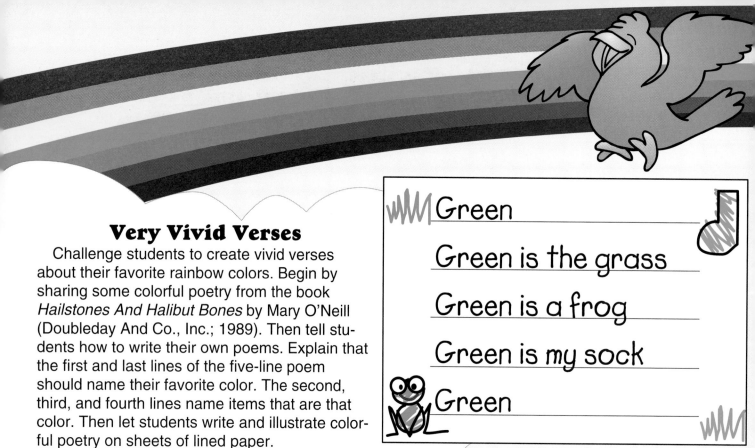

Very Vivid Verses

Challenge students to create vivid verses about their favorite rainbow colors. Begin by sharing some colorful poetry from the book *Hailstones And Halibut Bones* by Mary O'Neill (Doubleday And Co., Inc.; 1989). Then tell students how to write their own poems. Explain that the first and last lines of the five-line poem should name their favorite color. The second, third, and fourth lines name items that are that color. Then let students write and illustrate colorful poetry on sheets of lined paper.

Green

Green is the grass

Green is a frog

Green is my sock

Green

At Opposite Ends Of The Rainbow

Create this learning center for some extra antonym practice. Trace and cut out 10 rainbow patterns and 20 cloud patterns. Program ten of the cloud patterns with vocabulary words; program the other ten clouds with words that are the *opposite* of the words just written. To play the game, students find two words that are opposites and place one at each end of a rainbow. Vary this game for other matching skills such as synonyms, homonyms, words/abbreviations, and basic math facts/answers.

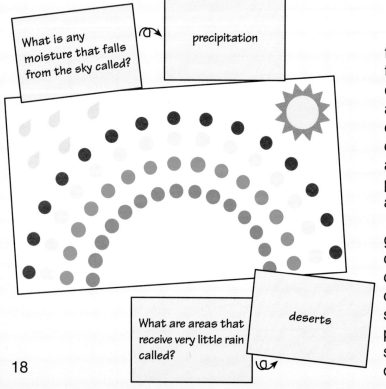

What is any moisture that falls from the sky called?

precipitation

What are areas that receive very little rain called?

deserts

Race Across The Rainbow

Create a quick and easy gameboard to reinforce "rainy" knowledge. Obtain a large piece of tagboard and red, yellow, green, and blue sticky dots. Use 15 red dots to create a trail that arches from one end of the tagboard to the other. Repeat the process with the remaining colors of dots, forming a rainbow. Draw a sun and raindrops over the rainbow, if desired. Next program cards with weather-related questions and code the backs for self-checking.

To play, each student chooses a red, yellow, green, or blue marker and places it on the corresponding trail. Cards are placed in the center of the gameboard. Each child in turn chooses a card, reads the question, and answers it. If the child answers correctly, he flips a penny and moves one space for heads or two spaces for tails. The first player to reach the end of his trail wins!

Drip-Drop Art

Persuade pupils to paint pretty pointillistic pictures! Explain that pointillism is the art of applying small dots to a surface so that from a distance they appear to blend together. Then provide each student with a large piece of white construction paper, cotton swabs, and colored tempera paints. To create pictures, have students use their cotton swabs to dab the paints on their papers. After the paintings are dry, display them on a bulletin board with the title "Pretty Pointillistic Paintings."

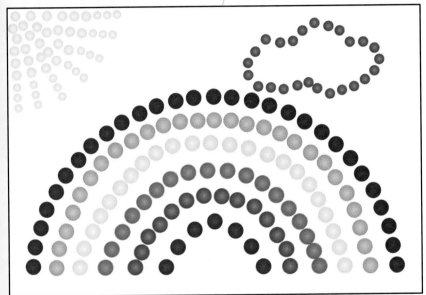

Pasta Rainbows

Create "pasta-tively" delightful rainbows with your students! Obtain large pasta wheels and color them in a mixture of rubbing alcohol and food coloring, so that they correspond to the colors of the rainbow. When the pasta wheels have dried overnight, distribute an assortment of colored pasta, glue, and a 5" x 7" piece of waxed paper to each student. Instruct each student to cover her waxed paper with glue. Have the student set the red pasta wheels in the glue to form the top layer of her rainbow. She should continue in this manner until she has used each of the different colors of pasta. After the glue has dried overnight, have each student remove her project from the waxed paper. Attach a piece of string through the rainbow and suspend it from the classroom ceiling.

Suncatcher Creations

Use colorful displays to bring rainbows indoors! To make a rainbow, each student will need two 5" x 12" pieces of waxed paper, crayon shavings (corresponding to each color of the rainbow), white construction paper, cotton, string, scissors, glue, and a copy of a rainbow pattern. (An iron will also be used by an adult.)

Instruct each student to use his pattern to trace a rainbow on one of the sheets of waxed paper. Then instruct each student to bring the waxed paper to a table that has been covered with towels. Make containers of shaved crayons available. Show the student how to sprinkle the appropriate colors of crayon shavings in the correct bands on the rainbow. Then place the second piece of waxed paper on the first, and gently press with an iron. When the rainbow is cool, instruct each student to cut it out. Have the student use his construction paper to make cloud cutouts. Cover the clouds with cotton for a more realistic appearance and glue to each end of the rainbow. Tape students' creations to classroom windows.

The Rainbow Fish

Share the story *The Rainbow Fish* by Marcus Pfister (North-South Books, 1992). This story describes a little fish and his quest for friendship. Make a splash with students when you show them how to create their own rainbow fish! Provide each student with a copy of the patterns on page 22, four coffee filters, and cups of water that have been tinted with food coloring to correspond to the colors of the rainbow. Instruct students to cut out their fish and scale patterns.

Then create rainbow-colored scales that will be glued to the fish. Instruct each student to fold her filters into eighths. Dip the edges of the filters into the food coloring, creating a tie-dyed effect. Unfold and let dry for approximately 30 minutes. Then, using the pattern, trace scales on the filters and cut them out. Glue the scales onto the fish, working from the back of the fish to the front so that they overlap one another. Display the fishy friends on a classroom bulletin board titled "Color Your World With Friendship." On a scale of one to ten—this activity rates a ten!

Name _____

Write Me A Rainbow

How do different colors make you feel?
Do certain colors remind you of different things?
Write your ideas on the lines below.

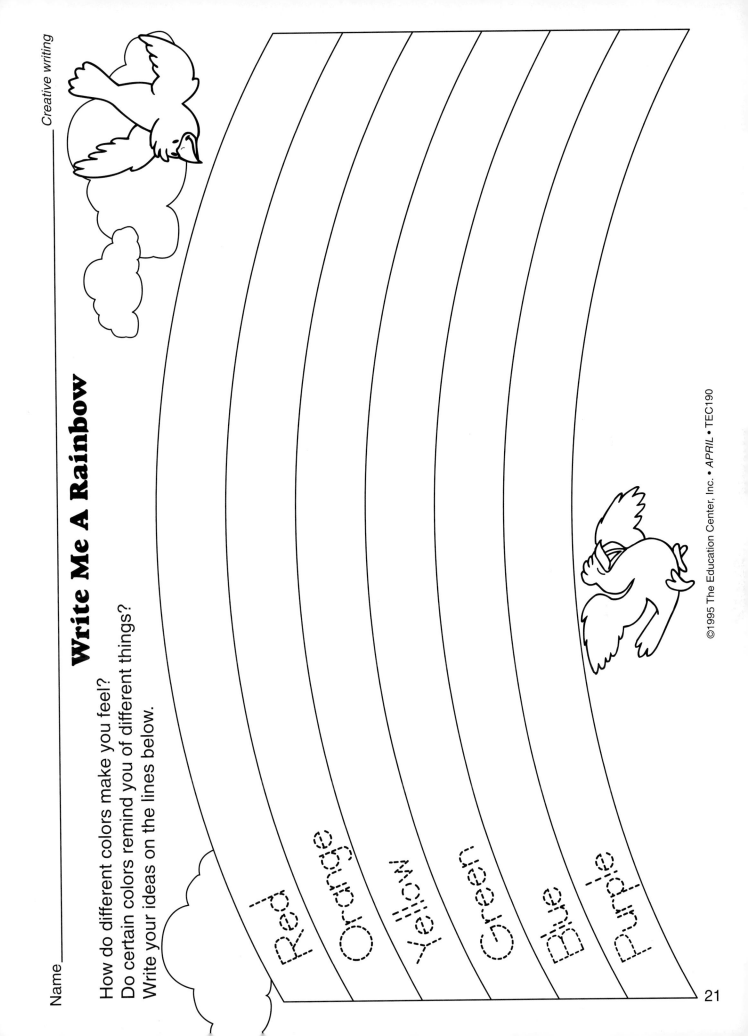

Red

Orange

Yellow

Green

Blue

Purple

21

Patterns
Use with "The Rainbow Fish" on page 20.

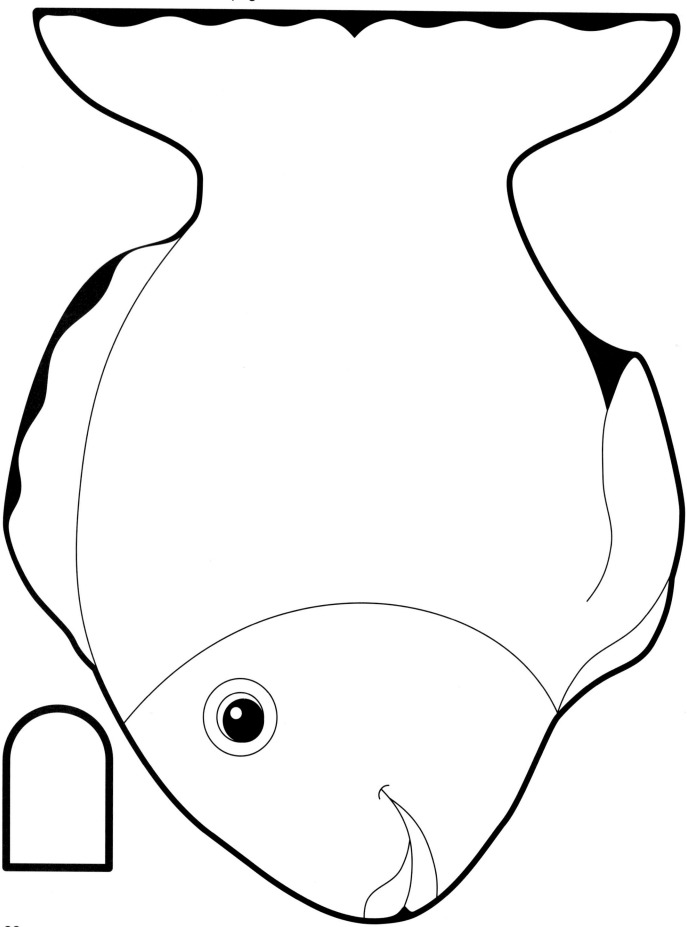

Celebrate A Rainy Day!

Celebrate learning in splashy style!

Rainbow Jell-O®

Create this colorful creation by preparing several packages of Jell-O®, as directed. When the Jell-O® is ready, cut it into cubes, place in cups, and distribute to students along with spoons. Top each with a whipped-cream cloud and enjoy!

Torrents Of Rainy-Day Fun

Culminate your unit on raindrops and rainbows by inviting other classes to your room to see what students have learned! Have students share their poems, stories, experiment booklets, art projects, and general knowledge of raindrops and rainbows with their peers. Wrap up your celebration by sharing rainbow cookies and punch with the other students.

A Rainbow Of A Salad!

Make a colorful snack with students! Brainstorm with students fruits that correspond to the colors of the rainbow (such as green kiwi, yellow bananas, purple grapes, blueberries, etc.) and list them on the board. Then enlist students' help in making a rainbow fruit salad. Provide, or have students provide, the ingredients to make the colorful dish. After all the ingredients have been cleaned, cut, and combined, it's time to consume! Distribute cups of fruit salad along with spoons and enjoy.

A Rainy-Day Relay

Brighten students' spirits with this relay race. Divide students into teams. Have each team make a line to prepare for the relay race. Provide the first child in each line with a raincoat, boots or galoshes, and an umbrella. That child puts on the coat and boots, then runs with the closed umbrella to a predetermined spot. He then turns around and runs back to his team. He passes the items to the next member of his team, who repeats the process. The team that completes this activity first wins!

Follow The Reading Rainbow

Rain Talk

by Mary Serfozo

(Macmillan Children's Book Group, 1990)

This story's poetic text and lovely illustrations depict the sights and sounds of a rainy day. Discuss the meanings of various rainy-day words such as *sprinkle, drizzle, downpour, cloudburst, and torrent.* Then have students use their bodies to create an indoor rainstorm. Simulate sprinkles by having students lightly tap their fingers on their desks. To simulate a drizzle, have students rub their hands together. To create a downpour, have students pat their hands on their legs, creating the sound of a summer shower.

Mud Puddle

by Robert Munsch

(Firefly Books, Ltd.; 1982)

Some children may not like rain—but many certainly like the results! Share the story *Mud Puddle* with your students. In this story a little girl is bothered by a mud puddle, until she thinks of a clever way to get rid of it! Ask students if they like to play in mud puddles and why. Then encourage students to create their own mud-puddle pictures.

Provide each student with a large sheet of finger-painting paper and brown finger paint. Encourage students to use the paint to create large mud puddles on their papers. When these have dried, have students draw pictures of children playing in the mud puddles!

Mushroom In The Rain

by Mirra Ginsburg

(Macmillan Children's Books, 1987)

Share the story *Mushroom In The Rain* with students. In this tale, an increasing number of animals seek shelter from the rain under a mushroom, and the fabulous fungus grows to accommodate them. Encourage students to dramatize this story. Ask one volunteer to portray the mushroom by standing and holding his arms out at shoulder height. Select other volunteers to portray the animals that find shelter under the mushroom. Brainstorm and list names of other animals that could find shelter under the mushroom.

Then let students create their own mushroom pictures! Provide each student with a piece of white construction paper, half of a large mushroom (cut vertically), a small container of brown paint, and crayons. Instruct each student to dip his mushroom half into his paint and then onto his paper, forming a mushroom print. Have the student draw pictures of animals that are seeking protection from the rain under the mushroom. Complete the picture by drawing a rainy-day scene around the mushroom and animals. Challenge older students to write sentences telling about their pictures. Bind completed work into a class collection called "The Marvelous Mushroom."

It's Raining Books And More Books!

Rain Drop Splash by Alvin Tresselt (Lothrop, Lee And Shepard, Company; 1966)

What Makes It Rain?: The Story Of A Raindrop by Keith Brandt (Troll Associates, 1982)

Rain And Hail by Franklyn Branley (Crowell, 1983)

Listen To The Rain by Bill Martin, Jr., and John Archambault (Henry Holt And Company, 1988)

Planting A Rainbow by Lois Ehlert (Harcourt Brace Jovanovich And Company, 1988)

A Bear In The Air by Leslie Williams (Stemmer House Publishers, Inc.; 1979)

The Tale Of The Vanishing Rainbow by Siegfried Rupprecht (North-South Books, 1989)

The Water's Journey by Eleonore Schmid (North-South Books, 1989)

Hooray For Hans!

Use the fabulous fairy tales of
Hans Christian Andersen to celebrate
the author's birthday on April 2.

An Extraordinary Man

Hans Christian Andersen was born on April 2, 1805, in one of the poorest sections of Odense, Denmark. Although money was not plentiful, Andersen was rich in the love and encouragement given to him by his family. As an only child, he spent most of his time alone and preferred it that way. He filled his hours listening to his grandmother's folktales, playing with the many toys his father made for him, and making doll clothes for the puppets he would use to act out plays. He also enjoyed singing and reciting plays in public.

In fact, he so loved performing that he decided to leave home at the age of 14 to seek fame as an actor. He told his mother that he knew he was an extraordinary man who would become famous. He was correct on both counts. Luckily for generations of children and adults, storytelling rather than acting became his true calling. It is for his mystical, marvelous fairy tales that Hans Christian Andersen finally achieved the fame that he knew he would find.

The Ugly Duckling

In this sensitive tale, Andersen relays the story of a *cygnet,* or baby swan, that is mistakenly born to a family of ducks. Ostracized by other ducks because of his unattractive appearance, the Ugly Duckling sets out to find a place where he belongs. He spends a difficult winter alone, braving hardships. But in the spring he is transformed into a beautiful swan.

After hearing *The Ugly Duckling,* have youngsters create Ugly Duckling stick puppets. To prepare, duplicate a supply of duckling patterns from page 29. Provide each student with a duckling pattern on yellow construction paper, two wiggly eyes, glue, scissors, and a craft stick. To make a puppet, a student cuts out the duckling, glues wiggly eyes on the duckling's head, and glues the duckling to a craft stick. Encourage students to use their stick puppets to reenact the tale of *The Ugly Duckling.*

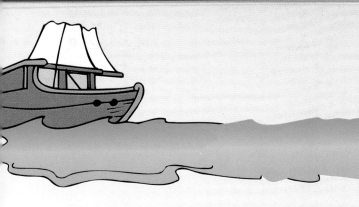

The Little Mermaid

A mermaid gives up her tail, her voice, and perhaps her life for the chance to be with her beloved prince. Students may be surprised to discover that, when retelling stories, professional writers often make changes to suit their needs. Sometimes an author even changes the outcome of a story that he is retelling. Give students an opportunity to see this for themselves by comparing the three versions of *The Little Mermaid* listed below. On chart paper, draw and label a grid as shown. Read aloud one version of the story; then ask students to help you complete the sections of the grid based upon that version. Repeat this process for each book. Lead students to notice the similarities and differences among the stories by comparing the information in the blocks of the grid. Then have students retell *The Little Mermaid* in their own words.

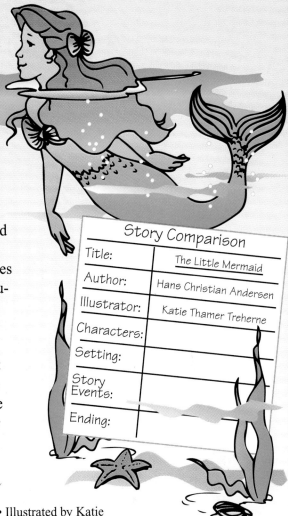

Story Comparison	
Title:	The Little Mermaid
Author:	Hans Christian Andersen
Illustrator:	Katie Thamer Treherne
Characters:	
Setting:	
Story Events:	
Ending:	

Bibliography

The Little Mermaid • Written by Hans Christian Andersen • Illustrated by Katie Thamer Treherne • Published by Harcourt Brace Jovanovich, Publishers; 1989

The Little Mermaid • Written by Hans Christian Andersen • Illustrated by Chihiro Iwasaki • Published by Picture Book Studio USA, 1984

Disney's The Little Mermaid • Written and Illustrated by the Walt Disney Staff • Published by Mouseworks, 1994

If I were a merman, I would swim with the fish all day and look for sunken treasures.

Bryan

My Life As A Mermaid

Sailors of old used to tell stories of mermaids—half-fish, half-human creatures that would lure ships onto dangerous rocks with their beautiful songs. After reading *The Little Mermaid,* encourage students to think about what it would be like to live as mermaids or mermen. Have each girl draw a picture of herself as a mermaid. Boys can draw themselves as mermen. Ask each child to write an undersea adventure that he or she might have as a merman or mermaid. Each story is sure to be a whale of a tale!

The Emperor's New Clothes

What happens when a very foolish Emperor meets some very crafty weavers? Well, the result could be an embarrassing fiasco—unless the Emperor can rise above the situation and clothe himself with dignity! Your youngsters will certainly feel some pity for the poor Emperor when he finds himself underdressed (to say the least!) in front of his subjects. Here's each youngster's chance to save the Emperor from humiliation. Discuss royal apparel. (Challenge older students to research the subject at the library.) After familiarizing your class with various styles and designs of royal regalia, reproduce the paper-doll pattern on page 29 for each child. Gather fabric scraps, buttons, sequins, ribbon, and a variety of other craft materials. Give each student a paper-doll pattern and a bottle of glue; then ask each child to select some craft materials and dress the Emperor in the finest clothes in his kingdom. After the dolls have been properly suited, sponsor a fashion show so that each Emperor can strut his new stuff!

Crown Jewels

The Emperor may have left the palace without his royal garments, but he would never have forgotten his crown! Your youngsters will have fun creating colorful crowns of their own. On tagboard reproduce a class supply of the crown pattern on page 30. For each child cut one 18" x 1 1/2" strip of tagboard to make a headband. Gather an assortment of faux jewels and several bottles of glitter glue. To make a crown, a student cuts out the crown pattern, colors the crown yellow or gold, and attaches faux jewels with glitter glue. If desired, a student can use the glitter glue to add shimmering highlights. Staple a headband strip to each crown and fit it to a child's head so that each child can wear her crown proudly.

Have youngsters parade through the hallways of their educational dominions. Then challenge each child to truly experience leadership by writing down five laws that she would pass in her own kingdom. Have each child share aloud her laws and her reasons for wishing to enact them.

Bibliography

The Emperor's New Clothes • Written by Hans Christian Andersen • Retold and Illustrated by Nadine Bernard Westcott • Published by Little, Brown and Company; 1984

The Emperor's New Clothes • Written by Hans Christian Andersen • Retold by Ruth Belov Gross • Illustrated by Jack Kent • Published by Four Winds Press, 1977

The Emperor's New Clothes • Written by Hans Christian Andersen • Adapted and Illustrated by Janet Stevens • Published by Holiday House, Inc.; 1985

The Ugly Duckling • Written by Hans Christian Andersen • Retold by Adrian Mitchell • Illustrated by Jonathan Heale • Published by Dorling Kindersley Publishing, Inc.; 1994

The Ugly Duckling • Written by Hans Christian Andersen • Retold and Illustrated by Troy Howell • Published by G. P. Putnam's Sons, 1990

The Ugly Duckling • Written by Hans Christian Andersen • Illustrated by Jennie Williams • Published by Troll Associates, 1979

Patterns

Use with *The Ugly Duckling* on page 26.

Use with *The Emperor's New Clothes* on page 28.

Patterns

Use with "Crown Jewels" on page 28.

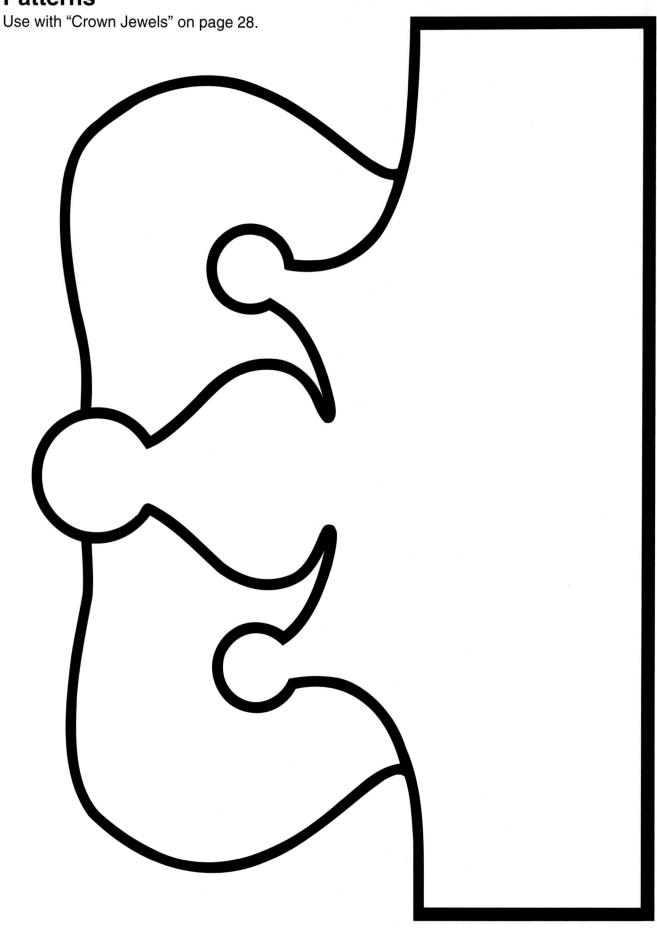

30

The Endangered Earth

Earth Day has been observed on April 22 of each year since 1970. Plan a unit to inform students about environmental issues such as endangered species and resource conservation. From recycling to rain forests, your students are sure to get involved with these planetary projects!

There's No Place On Earth I'd Rather Be

Let music set the mood by teaching your students the traditional song, "I Love The Mountains." (If your students are up to it, have them try singing this song in a round.) Then ask students to think of a place on Earth that they love, such as on the beach, in the mountains, under a favorite tree in the park, or in their backyard. Have students draw or paint pictures of their chosen spots. Mount the finished illustrations on colored construction-paper backgrounds, label each with the location depicted, and display them on a bulletin board titled "The Best Places On Earth."

I Love The Mountains
Traditional

I love the mountains, I love the rolling hills,
I love the fountains, I love the daffodils,
I love the fireside when all the lights are low;
Boom-ti-a-da, boom-ti-a-da,
Boom-ti-a-da, boom-ti-ay!

The Big Blue Marble

Help students develop a better understanding of planet Earth with this model art project. Begin by showing students some photographs of Earth from space, observing the colors. Ask students to speculate why Earth has nicknames such as The Blue Planet and The Big Blue Marble. Explain that oceans cover about 70 percent of Earth's surface, which accounts for all the blue they see. Help students determine that the patches of white are clouds, wrapping around the planet like a blanket. Explain that Earth is surrounded by an *atmosphere* of air, which allows our planet to sustain life. Lastly observe the shape of Earth. Although it appears round in photos, Earth is actually flattened out at the two poles and it bulges slightly at the equator. (The shape of the balloon in the art project that follows approximates this shape.)

After your discussion, have students create papier-mâché models of Earth. For each student, inflate a small balloon and tie it closed. Prepare a thin paste of flour and water, and provide a large supply of newspaper strips. Have each child dip newspaper strips in the paste, then cover the balloon completely. Be sure to have students overlap the layers, so that none of the balloon is showing. Allow the papier-mâché to dry for about two days, until it is hard. After drying, carefully cut off the tied end of the balloon and let it deflate inside the shell. Pull the balloon out through the hole. Then allow students to paint their models with tempera paints. Provide green and brown (for land), blue (for water), and white (for clouds). When dry, suspend the Earth models from your classroom ceiling to set the mood for the remainder of your Earth Day unit.

Gee... it looks just like me!

31

What's It All About?

When students have had a chance to reflect on their planet, both up close and faraway, lead a discussion about Earth Day and why it's observed each year. Make a list of what Earth provides for humans: water, food, air, energy, and shelter. Then assist students in listing some threats to the environment, such as pollution, deforestation, overflowing landfills, and acid rain. Divide students into small groups and assign each group an environmental problem to research. Have groups give oral presentations on what they learn. If all the problems leave your students feeling overwhelmed, read some ideas from John Javna's *50 Simple Things Kids Can Do To Save The Earth* (Andrews and McMeel, 1990). Then gear up for some Earth-saving activities!

The Planet Pledge

Create a bulletin board with environmental energy! Duplicate the paper-topper pattern on page 37 for each student. Have each child write one thing she plans to do to help save the Earth on a sheet of writing paper. Let students color the paper toppers and glue them to their writings. Display the papers on a bulletin board with the title "Take The Planet Pledge!"

Letting The Trash Out Of The Bag

Introduce the topic of recycling with this hands-on activity. To prepare, save all your trash at home (without removing recyclable materials) for about three days. Bring your trash to school, and have students weigh it and determine the amount of space the bag of trash takes up in cubic inches. Then have students wear rubber gloves and sort through the trash, removing all items that can be recycled, such as cans, cardboard, plastic containers, glass, newspaper, and other paper. Then have students weigh the trash again and determine its reduced space consumption. Discuss the value of recycling to save space in landfills. Read *Trash!* by Charlotte Wilcox (Carolrhoda Books, Inc.; 1988) for a closer look at what happens to the trash we throw away.

32

Who Recycles— And How?

How about a garbage-day graphing activity? Duplicate and send home the recycling checklist on page 38 for each student to complete for homework. Then create a class graph on a large sheet of bulletin-board paper to show what your students' families recycle. Cut a supply of index cards in half lengthwise. Have each child take the number of card strips equal to the number of recycling items checked on his paper. Have the children label the strips with their names, then mount them on the graph in the appropriate columns. When the graph is complete, compare the results by asking some questions such as the following: "Which item is most commonly recycled? Which is least? How many more [less] students recycle newspaper than aluminum cans?"

A Conservation Conversation

Recycling is one way to reduce the amount of trash in landfills; conservation is another. Show students how they can conserve materials with this simple demonstration. Place two lunches side by side on a table for students to observe. Pack one lunch in a paper bag with a paper napkin and several items wrapped in plastic wrap or plastic bags. Include a drink in a disposable container. Pack the other lunch in a reusable cloth or thermal bag or lunchbox. Put in a cloth napkin and several items in reusable plastic containers with lids. Include a drink in a thermos or plastic drink bottle.

Lead a discussion with students about these two options for lunch packaging. Ask students to consider the amount of trash that might be generated by your school during one lunch period if everyone used disposable wrappers and containers. What if everyone used plastic containers and cloth napkins instead? Point out that some disposable items (such as paper bags and plastic bags) can be reused a few times. Ask students to write a follow-up paragraph addressed to their parents explaining the demonstration.

We Are Not Alone

Of course, humans are not the only living things who need the Earth and its resources to stay alive. Plants and animals need a healthy planet for their survival, too. And many animals and plants are threatened, endangered, or extinct due to changes in the balance of nature—sometimes caused by humans.

To better explain the concepts of *endangered species* and *extinction,* play this game with your students. Designate one student to be your assistant; then seat all the others in a circle on the carpet. Explain that the seated students represent members of an imaginary species of animal. Your student assistant will portray humankind and their effects on this animal population. Have your assistant walk around the outer perimeter of the circle, tapping each student on the head and repeating, "Going, going, gone," stating one word as he taps each child. Each student who is tapped on the word *gone* gets up and leaves the circle. Stop the game when about one-half of the students are left in the circle. Explain that your imaginary animal species is now *threatened.* Continue the game until one-fourth of the students are left in the circle. Stop and explain that the species is now *endangered.* Let your assistant continue until all students have left the circle. Explain that your imaginary animal species is now *extinct.*

What's Happening In The Rain Forest?

In the forefront of endangered environments is the tropical rain forest. Acquaint your students with this fast-disappearing habitat by sharing *Rain Forest* by Helen Cowcher (Scholastic Inc., 1988). Take a picture walk through the first few pages of the book before reading the text. Ask students to describe what they see on those pages. Then tell students that in this story, something is frightening the animals and ask them to predict what it might be. Read the text aloud and discuss the ending of the story. Tell students that rain forests once covered 20 percent of Earth's land surface. They now cover only 6 or 7 percent. Ask students to write and illustrate continuations of Cowcher's story. Let students share their writings and illustrations. Compare positive and negative scenarios envisioned by the students.

Tropical Products

Many products that we use every day originated in the rain forest. For homework, ask students to fill out the checklist on page 39 to show which rain forest products they can find in their homes. Bring in a few of the more unusual food items, such as *guavas* or *plantains,* to show to students who may be unfamiliar with them. Point out that when people buy rain forest items that can be sustainedly harvested, such as cashews, this gives people living in rain forest regions a reason to preserve the rain forests.

Rain Forest Recipes

After discussing their completed homework assignments, treat students to a snack of Rain Forest Treat. Mix together two cups each of mixed nuts, chocolate chips, dried banana chips, and shredded coconut. While students are snacking, distribute a blank index card to each student. Challenge students to write and illustrate their own recipes using some food items from the rain forest products lists. Compile the recipe cards and add a cover labeled "Rain Forest Recipes" to create a mini cookbook for your classroom.

33

To Whom It May Concern

Practice letter-writing skills with a planetary purpose! Invite students to write letters to lawmakers, requesting their assistance with a local or global environmental issue of students' choice. Here are the addresses for your congressional representatives:

Honorable _____
U.S. House Of Representatives
Washington, DC 20515

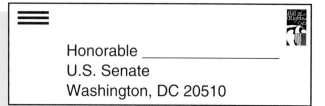

Honorable _____
U.S. Senate
Washington, DC 20510

Conservation Is Catching On!

Brainstorm other ways to conserve natural resources. Challenge students to list ways to conserve water (turn off the faucet while brushing teeth), paper (clean up spills with sponges instead of paper towels), and energy (turn off the lights whenever you leave a room). Have each student choose a conservation tip, write a catchy phrase to convey it to others, and then create a poster featuring her phrase and an illustration. Display the posters in your school library or cafeteria.

Environmental Organizations

Here are just a few organizations you can contact for educational materials and information on preservation of the Earth and its animals.

The Nature Conservancy
1815 North Lynn Street
Arlington, VA 22209
1-703-841-4860
(Adopt An Acre program to preserve an acre of tropical rain forest)

American Forests
Sharing in a Better World
P.O. Box 2000
Washington, DC 20013
1-800-545-TREE (8733)
(Tree-planting program)

Save The Manatee® Club
Adopt-A-Manatee Program
500 North Maitland Avenue
Maitland, FL 32751
1-800-432-JOIN (5646)
(Adoption of endangered manatees)

International Wildlife Coalition
Whale Adoption Project
70 East Falmouth Highway
East Falmouth, MA 02536-5954
(Adoption of humpback whales)

An Earth Day Fair

Promote environmental awareness with a schoolwide celebration of Earth Day!
Enlist the help of families and administrators to hold an Earth Day Fair to get
your school and community in the Save-The-Earth spirit.

Dressing For The Occasion

Environmental messages will suit your students to a *T* with this activity. A week or two before your Earth Day Fair, have each student bring in a plain, white T-shirt from home. Provide bright colors of fabric paint in squeeze bottles, fabric paint brushes, and several T-shirt painting boards (available at craft stores). Let students decorate their T-shirts with Earth Day messages or tips for preserving the environment. Allow the shirts to dry for one or two days. Then have everyone suit up in their E-Team shirts on the day of your fair!

Earth Day Earnings

Have students plan to sell something at the fair to help raise money for an environmental cause. Allow students to choose a nonprofit organization to make a donation to, such as a fund for aiding an endangered species or a preservation fund for a tropical rain forest. (See the box on page 34 for more information on specific causes.) A bake sale is a tried-and-true fundraiser. Or, if your school has access to the machinery, you could sell popcorn or sno-cones. Have students create advertising posters explaining their products, prices, and distribution of profits. If your school has an in-house video system, get students involved in preparing and producing a broadcast to let other students know about the fair and items for sale.

Recycling Stations

Your fair can promote good recycling habits in the neighborhood by providing recycling stations for various items. Have families bring in their newspapers, aluminum cans, phone books, or magazines. Have students man various recycling stations, and ask parent volunteers to help the class transport the items to local recycling centers. If you live in an area where money is paid for recyclables, add the income from recycling to your environmental fund.

Trash To Treasures

Promote conservation at your fair by running a toy swap or book swap. Children can bring in their old toys or books and exchange them with someone else. Everything old is new again—to someone else!

Hands-On Earth Activities

Get fair-goers involved with hands-on activities to help the Earth! Set up a station where folks can stop and participate for a short while in an Earth-caring activity. This could be as simple as cutting apart the plastic rings from six-pack containers (to lessen the danger to animals). Or you could set up a station where participants spread pinecones with peanut butter and roll them in inexpensive birdseed to create bird feeders for a local park. Or provide opportunities to beautify school grounds by planting flowers or doing repair work on a school playground. You'll be amazed at how much gets accomplished!

Stories From A Small Planet

Share these literature selections to extend your students'
experiences with Earth Day and environmental issues.

For The Love Of Our Earth
by P. K. Hallinan
(Ideals Children's Books, 1992)

This simple, poetic book is full of positive messages
encouraging children to care for the planet in numerous
ways, from planting trees to being kind to one another.
After sharing it with your students, invite them to create
their own poetic plans for bettering the world. Let them
illustrate their finished verses and display the completed
work on a bulletin board titled "Poems For The Planet."

Welcome To The Green House
by Jane Yolen
(Scholastic Inc., 1993)

Beautiful illustrations by Laura Regan make this book a
must-read when learning about the rain forest. After a first
reading, review each page with your students and discuss
the beautiful plant and animal life depicted. Then involve
students in creating a rain forest mural for your classroom
or hallway. Provide the class with long lengths of white
bulletin-board paper, brushes, pencils, and a variety of
colors of tempera paint. Be sure to mix several shades of
green tempera paint. Encourage students to use pencils
to sketch out their scenes, then paint using the brushes.
You might also provide colored construction paper or
tissue paper and glue to give a mixed-media look to the
mural. Your creative students are sure to produce a
dazzling version of the "green house"!

Sam The Sea Cow
by Francine Jacobs
(Walker and Company, 1979)

Introduce your students to an endangered animal with
this story based on the real-life rescue of a Florida
manatee. Manatees are in danger of extinction due to
speeding motorboats and polluted waters—products of
humankind's encroachment on the manatees' habitat.
After sharing the story and discussing this endangered
animal, invite your students to research other endangered animals and complete the research form on page
40.

Heron Street
by Ann Turner
(Scholastic Inc., 1989)

Your students will find a mini American-history lesson
in this story about the effects of the settlement and
growth of our country on the natural environment. Ann
Turner uses many descriptive sound words, such as
"sqwonk," "sputter-pop," and "chirr-whirr" to relate the
sounds of animals and machines. Challenge students
to create each of the sound effects in the story—either
with their voices or by using props. Then do a choral
reading of the story, inserting the sound effects. Perform the choral reading for another class. Follow up
with a discussion of noise pollution. Do your students
think this is as serious a problem as air or water pollution? Why or why not?

More Love-The-Earth Literature

The Earth And I
by Frank Asch
(Harcourt, Brace and Company; 1994)

World, World, What Can I Do?
by Barbara S. Hazen
(Morehouse Publishing, 1991)

Will We Miss Them?
by Alexandra Wright
(Charlesbridge Publishing, 1991)

Where The Forest Meets The Sea
by Jeannie Baker
(Greenwillow Books, 1987)

Journey Of The Red-Eyed Tree Frog
by Tanis Jordan
(Green Tiger Press, 1992)

Dinosaurs To The Rescue!: A Guide To Protecting Our Planet
by Laurie K. Brown & Marc Brown
(Little, Brown, and Company; 1992)

The Great Trash Bash
by Loreen Leedy
(Holiday House, Inc.; 1991)

My Pledge For The Planet...

Glue paper here.   ©1995 The Education Center, Inc. • *APRIL* • TEC 190

My Pledge For The Planet...

Glue paper here.   ©1995 The Education Center, Inc. • *APRIL* • TEC 190

The Recycling Routine

Check the items that are regularly recycled at your house.

❑ newspaper

❑ aluminum cans

❑ plastic

❑ glass

❑ tin cans

❑ cardboard

❑ phone books

❑ magazines

❑ clothing passed to younger children or given away

❑ yard wastes (made into mulch)

❑ compost

❑ other: _____

_____

_____

Note To The Teacher: Use this reproducible with "Who Recycles – And How?" on page 32.

Fruits Of The Rain Forest

Many foods, spices, and other products come from the tropical rain forest.
Check the items below that you find in your home.

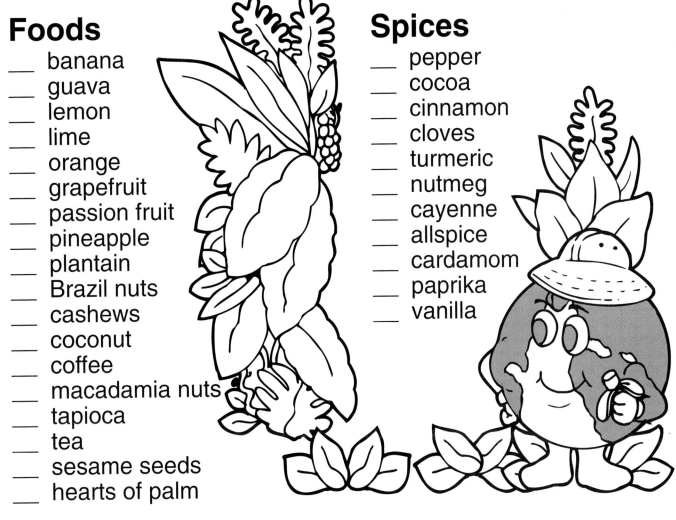

Foods

___ banana
___ guava
___ lemon
___ lime
___ orange
___ grapefruit
___ passion fruit
___ pineapple
___ plantain
___ Brazil nuts
___ cashews
___ coconut
___ coffee
___ macadamia nuts
___ tapioca
___ tea
___ sesame seeds
___ hearts of palm

Spices

___ pepper
___ cocoa
___ cinnamon
___ cloves
___ turmeric
___ nutmeg
___ cayenne
___ allspice
___ cardamom
___ paprika
___ vanilla

Other

___ camphor oil (insect repellent)
___ coconut oil (foods, lotions, soaps)
___ palm oil (foods)
___ chicle (gum base)

Note To Teacher: Use this reproducible with "Tropical Products" on page 33.

An Animal In Danger!
Research Report

This endangered animal is a _____ .

Here is a picture of it:

[ ]

It lives _____ .

It eats _____ .

An interesting thing about this animal is _____

_____

_____ .

It is endangered because _____

_____

_____ .

Some ways to help save this animal are _____

_____

_____

_____ .

Note To The Teacher: Use this reproducible with *Sam The Sea Cow* on page 36.

Trees Are Terrific!

Celebrate springtime and National Arbor Day by focusing on the beauty and benefits of trees.

Hello, Trees!

Begin your study of trees by meeting some of the locals! Take a walk on your school grounds or in your neighborhood to let students view trees. Encourage students to verbalize what they see. Ask questions such as "What is happening to the trees at this time of year? Do the leaves on all trees look the same? Do you know the names of any of these trees? What do you like best about trees?" Then return to your classroom and print two headings on a large sheet of chart paper: "What We Think We Know About Trees" and "What We Want To Know About Trees." Record student responses under the two headings. Keep the chart available in your classroom throughout your study. Record the answers to student questions and make corrections to student beliefs as you learn more about the topic of trees.

Forest Favorites

Share the beautiful verse and illustrations of *Have You Seen Trees?* by Joanne Oppenheim (Scholastic Inc., 1995). The last section of the book describes many types of trees—from ash trees to weeping willows—and tells how each type of tree is used by people.

After sharing the book, duplicate a copy of page 49 for each student. Have each child choose a favorite tree and write about why she likes it best. Have her add an illustration of her tree, using Oppenheim's book or a simple tree guide as a reference. Display the finished pages on a bulletin board with the title "A Few Favorites From The Forest." To add a mathematical dimension to this activity, create a bar graph to illustrate the number of students who chose each type of tree.

A Tree For All Seasons

Create a bulletin board of "tree-mendous" proportions! Read the story *The Seasons Of Arnold's Apple Tree* by Gail Gibbons (Harcourt Brace Jovanovich, 1984). Discuss with students the variations in *deciduous trees* during each of the four seasons. Then divide the class into four groups and assign each group one season. Provide each group with a large, identical cutout of a tree trunk and branches cut from brown bulletin-board paper. Have students in each group transform their tree to depict their assigned season, following the suggestions below and adding any creative touches they wish:

Winter—Cut snowflakes from white paper to add to the tree branches.
Spring—Tear leaves from light green tissue paper and crumple pastel tissue paper to make buds and flowers.
Summer—Cut leaves from shiny green wrapping paper.
Fall—Cut leaves from manila paper. Sponge-paint them with red, orange, and yellow tempera paint. Glue some to the branches and some at the base of the tree's trunk.

Display the four trees on a bulletin board with the title "A Tree For All Seasons." Print the season names on sentence strips and add a label below each tree.

In Celebration Of Trees

Tree-planting holidays are celebrated in countries all over the world. Holidays such as Greening Week (Japan), New Year's Day Of The Trees (Israel), Students' Afforestation Day (Iceland), and Tree-Loving Week (Korea) demonstrate that trees are important to people everywhere.

Most states in America celebrate National Arbor Day on the last Friday in April. (Check with a local agricultural extension agent to see when your state Arbor Day celebration occurs; dates vary due to planting conditions and weather.) Share the history of this holiday with your students by reading *Arbor Day* by Diane L. Burns (Carolrhoda Books, Inc.; 1989). Explain that J. Sterling Morton began Arbor Day in Nebraska in 1872. Morton wanted to encourage good *stewardship* of the earth. Discuss this word and its meaning with your students. Then have students tell what they can do to be good caretakers of the planet and its trees. Duplicate a "Tree Friend" badge on page 48 for each student to color, and take home.

OU LIKE TO SEE WHAT ES FROM A TREE?

paper cardboard my desk

What "Wood" We Do Without Trees?

Brainstorm with your students a list of the benefits of trees. Be sure to include the following: beauty, shade, oxygen, absorption of carbon dioxide, reduction of air and noise pollution, food and shelter for animals, prevention of erosion, food for humans, natural mulch, and provision of raw materials. Ask students to imagine what their daily lives might be like without trees. Ask each student to go on a hunt in your classroom and list five items that came from trees (such as pencils, desks, chairs, notebook paper, books, doors, shelving, paneling, posters, or bulletin boards). Then work together to create a display of tree products. Provide students with magazines, scissors, and glue. Have them locate pictures of food or wood items from trees, and add these pictures to a large tree shape cut from bulletin-board paper. Display the completed tree on a classroom wall with the title " 'Wood' You Like To See What Comes From A Tree?"

"Be-Leaf" It Or Not

Share these amazing facts about trees with your students:

- It takes 17 trees to make one ton of paper.
- The oldest known trees are bristlecone pines growing in the Rocky Mountains. Some are estimated to be 6,000 years old!
- Cinnamon is made from the bark of a tree grown in India and Sri Lanka.
- The largest tree on earth grows in the Redwood National Park. It is taller than the Statue of Liberty and is over 600 years old!
- Trees help cool the air through a process known as *transpiration.* They take water in through their roots and release it as vapor through small holes in their leaves called *stomata.* A mature oak tree can release up to 300 gallons of water a day!
- One oak tree may have 400 species of plants and animals living on it.
- The smallest tree is the snow willow. It grows in the Arctic, in the cracks of rocks. Only a few inches high, its trunk is about as thin as a pencil.

Arbor Day Action

What better way to celebrate Arbor Day than by planting a tree? *Red Leaf, Yellow Leaf* by Lois Ehlert (Harcourt Brace & Co., 1991) is a good introduction to tree planting. After sharing the book with your class, have an arborist or a tree nursery worker come to visit your classroom. A professional can guide your students to consider the following before planting: climate, moisture, light and shade levels, local pest problems, soil make-up, and level of air pollution present—all important factors in matching a tree and an appropriate location. He can also help students envision the space necessary for the tree's roots and branches at maturity. Once you've chosen the location and the type of tree, contact a local nursery or agricultural extension agency about donating a seedling to your class. You might even be able to arrange for each student to receive a seedling to plant at home!

When your seedling has arrived, plan a tree-planting ceremony on or near Arbor Day. Invite parents or another class to attend. After your new tree is in place, celebrate by reading aloud *The Giving Tree* by Shel Silverstein (Harper and Row, 1964). Let each student share one thing she has learned about the beauty or benefits of trees to people. Then observe your tree daily to care for it and get to know it from trunk to twigs and bark to buds!

Looking At Leaves

Practice classification skills with some local leaves. Gather a variety of leaves from the trees in your area. Provide each student or cooperative pair with a zippered plastic bag containing several specimens. Ask students to examine the leaves and note likenesses and differences. Have them sort the leaves into groups by the criteria of their choice—size, shape, texture, etc. Ask them to glue two or more leaves to a sheet of manila paper as examples from their groups. Have students share their examples with the class, explaining their sorting criteria. Use the student examples as springboards to share information with the class about types of leaves. Discuss *needles* versus *broadleaves, simple leaves* versus *compound,* and *toothed edges* versus *smooth* or *lobed edges.* Provide examples for the class if no student examples are available.

Finish the lesson by choosing examples which clearly demonstrate each type of leaf division discussed (provided either by you or students). Label the examples and display them in your science center for student reference.

The Planting Plan

After your students have planted their new tree friend, return to the classroom for a writing experience. Ask students to carefully recall each step in planting the tree. For younger students, record their dictation on a large sheet of chart paper. When you and your students are satisfied with the sequence and clarity of the steps, recopy the sentences on a clean sheet. Then assign students to create simple drawings of each step on index cards. Attach the illustrations to the chart. If your students are taking home their own seedlings to plant, create a reduced version of the instructions and duplicate it for each student to take home. Have older students write and illustrate their own set of instructions on individual papers.

Branching Out In Math

Your students will enjoy these fun estimation activities using real trees. Have students work in groups of three. Each group should locate a mature tree in a fairly open area on your school grounds. Have each group fill in a duplicated copy of page 50 to report its findings.

Estimate the tree's height. One child stands about 60 feet from the tree's trunk (on level ground), holding a yardstick upright on the ground in front of him. Another child lies on her stomach about six feet from the first child. The student lying down looks at the spot where the top of the tree comes to on the yardstick and directs the standing child to mark that spot, telling him to move his hand up or down until she says, "Stop." The third child records the marked height in feet. Help the students multiply that height by ten to get the approximate height of the tree.

About 6 feet

About 60 feet

Estimate the tree's age. Use a tape measure to measure the circumference of the tree about five feet from the ground. Usually, a tree measures about one inch for each year of growth. If the tree is a pine, count the number of rows of branches radiating from the central trunk. Each row represents one year's growth.

Estimate the widest point of the *crown spread* (how far the branches spread from the trunk). The students determine which branch sticks out the farthest from the tree's trunk. The first child stands directly beneath that branch's tip. The second child walks to the side of the tree directly opposite and stands beneath the tip of that side's farthest branch. Then the two step out a few feet to one side of the tree, and the third child measures the distance between them.

Measure this distance.

trunk

top of tree

Tree Ring Writing

Your students will be fascinated to learn about the growth rings of a tree. If possible, obtain a real cross section of a tree for students to observe (sometimes fireplace logs are usable), or show students some pictures of growth rings from a nonfiction book about trees. Ask students to speculate why some rings are narrow and others wide or what might cause marks across the rings. Then explain that the rings are a record not only of the tree's age, but also of its health. Narrow rings denote a slow growth period, perhaps due to drought. Wide rings indicate a healthy year. Marks can be caused by fire, insect damage, or a fallen branch. If the rings are uneven or lopsided, this might indicate that the tree was growing on a slope or leaning away from a newly constructed building because of a lack of growth space.

Once students have discovered that a tree's rings tell its history, invite them to try this writing activity. Have each student draw a tree cross section equal in age to his own age. Have him label each ring with an event from that year in his life, beginning with his birth date at the center ring. Allow students to share their mini autobiographies with classmates.

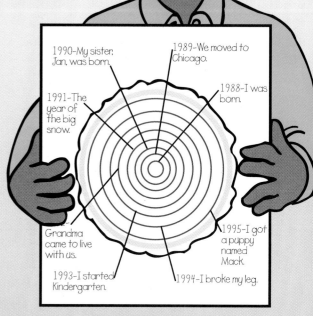

1990–My sister, Jan, was born.

1989–We moved to Chicago.

1991–The year of the big snow.

1988–I was born.

Grandma came to live with us.

1995–I got a puppy named Mack.

1993–I started Kindergarten.

1994–I broke my leg.

Tree Tees

Culminate your unit on trees by creating some wearable art! Ask each student to bring in a plain white T-shirt from home. Gather leaves in a variety of shapes and sizes; ask students to look on the ground for leaves that are still green. Then set up a work area with fabric paints, brushes, and T-shirt painting boards (available from a craft store). Each student should place a painting board inside her white T-shirt and smooth the surface. Have her choose several leaves to make an attractive design on the front of the shirt. Lightly coat one side of each leaf with paint and press them gently onto the T-shirt in the desired arrangement. If they wish, students can use the squeeze tips of the fabric paint bottles to write messages on the shirts, such as "Friend Of Trees" or "I Love Leaves!" When finished, the painting boards can be removed, but the shirts should be left lying flat to dry for a day or two, depending on the thickness of the paint. What trendy tree lovers!

Terrific Tales About Trees

Share these books to learn more about trees, leaves, and forests.

Tree Trunk Traffic

by Bianca Lavies
(E. P. Dutton, 1989)

Trees serve an important purpose as homes for many animals. Share this photo-illustrated book and make a list of all the animals depicted. (Can your students think of other tree-dwellers?) Then sketch out a large tree on a sheet of poster board or chart paper. Label your drawing "The Tree Hotel." Label one side of your drawing with the words *roots, trunk,* and *canopy.* Label the other side with the words *basement, first floor,* and *top floor.* Divide your class into three groups. Assign each group a floor of the tree hotel. Ask groups to draw or cut out pictures of animals that live on their floors. Reassemble your class and glue the pictures to the appropriate sections of the drawing.

A Busy Year

by Leo Lionni
(Alfred A. Knopf Books For Young Readers, 1992)

Two mice visit a tree friend during each month of the year in this delightful story. After a first read-through, review the illustrations on each page and allow students to comment on the changes they observe in the tree as the year progresses. Then have each student illustrate his own simplified version of the story in an accordion-folded book. For each student, cut three strips of white drawing paper, each 4" x 12". Use cellophane tape to connect the three strips; then accordion-fold the completed strip at three-inch intervals to create 12 sections. Turn the folded paper so that the top fold opens book-style. Using this as the book cover, have each student print a title and his name, and illustrate as desired. Then have him open out the folded strip and label the sections with the months of the year, in order. Have him illustrate a tree in each section, showing the appropriate changes or adding seasonal symbols for each month. Have students take the books home to share their seasonal knowledge!

Once There Was A Tree

by Natalia Romanova
(Dial Books, 1985)

Who owns a tree in the forest? This lovely book will get students thinking about our relationship with nature. Younger children can act out the story as the teacher reads aloud or older students can participate in a dramatic reading of the story with assigned parts. Perform the story either way for another class. Then share a discussion session with the audience about the message of the story.

The Big Tree
by Bruce Hiscock
(Atheneum, 1991)

This is the life story of a sugar maple tree in upstate New York—a tree that began as a seed at the time of the American Revolution and grew into a giant tree of today. Besides presenting general information about tree parts and growth, the book also explains the process of *sugaring,* or collecting sap to create maple sugar and maple syrup.

After sharing this story with your class, enjoy a treat of pancakes with real maple syrup! Follow the directions on the package of a commercial pancake mix and cook enough pancakes for everyone in your classroom, using an electric frying pan. Provide butter and syrup so students can enjoy yet another product from the terrific tree!

Badges
Use with "In Celebration Of Trees" on page 42.

A Forest Favorite

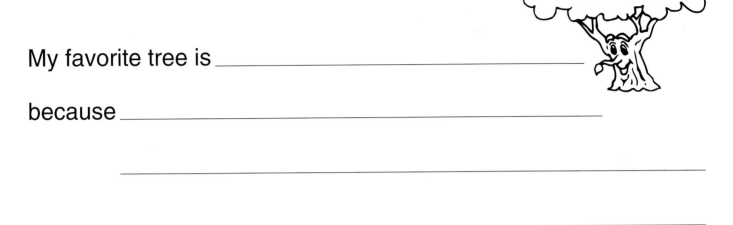

My favorite tree is _____

because _____

_____

_____

Here is a picture of my favorite tree:

The leaves look like this:

Note To The Teacher: Use this reproducible with "Forest Favorites" on page 41.

49

How Does Your Tree Measure Up?

Height:

_____ x 10 = _____

height recorded on
yardstick (in feet and inches)

estimated height
of tree

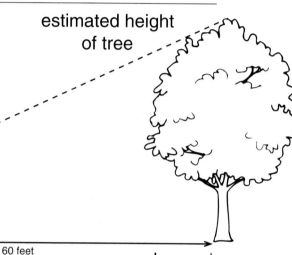

6 feet   60 feet

Age:

We measured _____ around the tree.
          inches

Our tree is approximately _____ years old.

Crown Spread:

We measured _____ at the widest
          feet, inches

point of the tree's crown.

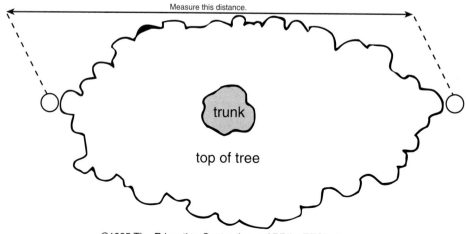

Measure this distance.

trunk

top of tree

It's An Easter "Eggs-travaganza"!

Bunnies and baskets and beautiful eggs—find them all in this
collection of fun ideas to celebrate the Easter season!

Bunny Tales

No doubt all of your students are familiar with the Easter Bunny. But each child probably has a different idea about this famous character's looks and behavior. Share several Easter Bunny–based stories, such as *The Big Bunny And The Easter Eggs* by Steven Kroll (Scholastic Inc., 1982), *The Country Bunny And The Little Gold Shoes* by Du Bose Heyward (Houghton Mifflin Company, 1967), and *Bunny Trouble* by Hans Wilhelm (Scholastic Inc., 1985). Have students compare and contrast these various depictions of the Easter Bunny. Discuss how Easter baskets were delivered in each story.

Then have your students write their own stories about the Easter Bunny, including descriptions of how the bunny completes his egg-delivery duties. Provide a variety of art materials so students can create their own illustrated versions of the famous rabbit. Display the students' completed stories on a bulletin board titled "Easter Bunny Escapades." Enlarge the Easter Bunny pattern on page 57 on poster board. Color and cut out the bunny; then use it as a centerpiece for the board. Duplicate copies of the egg pattern on page 57 on colored construction paper. Cut them out and use them as a border. Cut along the dotted line on the Easter Bunny's basket; then insert a few cutouts to finish the display.

51

Easter Around The World

Americans celebrate Easter with church services, Easter egg hunts, and the traditional baskets of goodies delivered by the Easter Bunny. But people in other countries have their own unique Easter traditions. Share these facts with your students and locate the countries where they take place on a map or globe.

—In Greece, people carry candles that are lighted at midnight services on Easter Eve. Many believe it is good luck to keep the candles burning until they reach home.

—In France, the church bells are silent from Good Friday until Easter morning. Legend has it that the bells are silent because they travel to Rome and then bring back gifts. On Easter morning, children rush outside to collect the candy and Easter eggs that have fallen from the sky.

—In Germany, many people believe it is good luck to eat a green food on the Thursday before Easter. Many Germans eat green salads on this day.

—In Australia, the seasons are the opposite of those in the Northern Hemisphere. While we are experiencing spring in America, Australians are greeting fall weather. Many Australians go camping during the Easter holidays.

—In Norway, people enjoy a five-day national holiday at Easter time. Many people go skiing at this time, and some ski trails have open-air chapels for worshipers.

Ask students which of these countries they might like to visit during the Easter season. Have them write about why they'd like to go there and what they would tell foreigners about American Easter traditions.

A-Hunting We Will Go

Your students will practice following directions when they participate in an Easter basket hunt. Divide your class into four or five groups. In advance, ask parent volunteers to help you prepare several large Easter baskets with treats such as candy, colored eggs, pencils, or other favors—one basket for each group. Hide the baskets in various locations around your school (with the informed help of school personnel such as a secretary, a media specialist, or other teachers). Then create a set of directions for each group to follow to locate its basket. If desired, make the hunt progressive by providing only one clue at a time, with a clue given at each new location. When all the groups have located their baskets, let them return to the classroom to enjoy the treats.

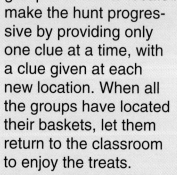

A Tisket, A Tasket

Your students will take to the task of creating these beautiful baskets. Provide each child with a small, inflated balloon and a supply of fabric squares cut with pinking shears. Mix up a batch of wheat paste (available at your local craft store). Have each student dip fabric squares into the paste to cover the bottom half of her balloon, being careful to layer and overlap the fabric squares so that no balloon shows through. Allow the paste to dry for one or two days; then deflate the balloons by carefully cutting off the knotted ends. Remove the balloons, leaving hardened fabric shells. To make a handle, have each child staple on a strip of colored construction paper.

Then plan a surprise visit from the Easter Bunny! While students are out of the room, fill each child's basket with commercial grass, jelly beans, and chocolate-candy eggs for a holiday surprise. Leave a note on the chalkboard that reads:

Hi, boys and girls!
I made an early visit to your classroom today! Have a "hoppy" Easter!
Love, the Easter Bunny

An "Eggs-tra" Special Tree

Add a beautiful dimension to your traditional egg-dyeing activities! Read aloud *The Egg Tree* by Katherine Milhous (Atheneum, 1981); then gather the necessary materials to create an egg tree for your classroom. Obtain a large branch and paint it white if desired. Anchor the branch securely in a large pot of sand or pebbles. Then have adult volunteers assist students in blowing out raw eggs. Each child should use a needle to poke a small hole in the narrow end of a raw egg and a slightly larger hole in the opposite end. Have him carefully blow air through the smaller hole, emptying the inside of the egg into a bowl. Rinse the eggs and allow them to dry overnight.

The following day, students can use egg dyes, watercolor paints, glitter pens, or tempera paints to decorate their hollow eggs. Have an adult use a hot glue gun to attach a loop of ribbon to the top of each egg. Hang your students' beautiful creations on your class egg tree for a delightful holiday decoration!

A Great Big Egg

Try some cooperative cooking to create an Easter treat. Provide your class with a roll of refrigerator sugar-cookie dough. Have student volunteers flatten the dough out on a pizza pan and pat it into the shape of a large Easter egg. Bake the giant cookie at the recommended temperature until golden brown. Then let students help to decorate the cooled cookie with various colors of icing, jelly beans, and colored sprinkles. Have students share their culinary creation while you read aloud the story *The Great Big Especially Beautiful Easter Egg* by James Stevenson (Scholastic Inc., 1983).

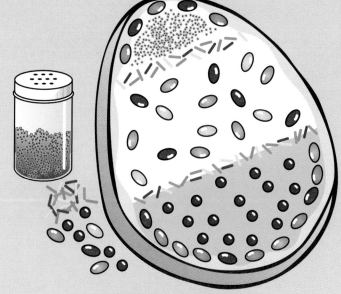

Funny Bunny

Make a bunny cake to celebrate the Easter season. Bake two round cake layers following the directions on the package. Let the cake cool; then use a sharp knife to cut one of the layers and assemble as shown. Frost the cake with vanilla icing; then sprinkle with coconut. Add jelly beans to resemble the nose and eyes. Use licorice strings to resemble the whiskers, and add other features such as the mouth and the ear outlines with pink tube frosting. Allow students to enjoy their cake while sharing the story *Rabbit Finds A Way* by Judy Delton (Crown Publishers, Inc.; 1975).

ear

tie

ear

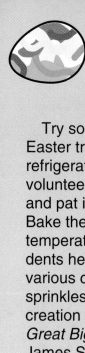

The Joys Of Jelly Beans

Jelly beans make memorable math manipulatives for these appetizing arithmetic activities! Don't forget to snack along the way!

Sorting And Graphing

Give each child a paper cup filled with jelly beans. Have her sort the jelly beans by color and fill in a copy of the graph on page 56. For more graphing fun, ask each child to choose her favorite color of jelly bean. Have her cut a jelly bean shape from a corresponding color of construction paper and label it with her name. Create a class graph on a large sheet of bulletin-board paper, and have students place their bean cutouts in the appropriate columns. Title the graph "On Which Bean Are You Keen?"

Addition And Subtraction

Make this jelly bean activity jump with compartmentalized plates from frozen dinners. To practice addition, provide each student with a plate, a supply of jelly beans, and some self-checking flash cards with addition problems. The child can place the number of jelly beans equal to each addend in one of the two smaller compartments, then transfer them to the larger compartment as he counts out the sum. He can check his work by turning over the flash card. To practice subtraction, use subtraction flash cards and follow the process in reverse.

Fractions

Give students practice with determining the fractional part of a set with this simple center. Obtain several film canisters and place a few jelly beans into each canister, taking care to put a varying number of pink jelly beans into each one. Have a student empty each canister in turn and determine what fractional part of the set is pink. To make the center self-checking, label the bottom of each canister with the correct answer.

Multiplication

Use jelly beans and cupcake liners to help students visualize multiplication facts. Tell students the cupcake liners are Easter baskets. Pose a sample problem such as "The Easter Bunny must deliver three baskets with four jelly beans in each one. How many jelly beans does he need?" Students should arrange three cupcake liners on their desks and fill each with four jelly beans. Have students count to figure out the total number of jelly beans. Write the multiplication problem on the board as a number sentence. Continue with other word problems or number sentences.

Estimation

Fill a medium-sized jar with jelly beans. Ask students to estimate the number of jelly beans in the jar. Place the jar where each child can observe it up close. Draw a number line on your chalkboard and record each child's estimate on the line. To check the answer, empty the jar and have groups of students count and add to find the total number of jelly beans. Find the closest estimate. Explore a multitude of math concepts by asking questions such as "Which estimate was the farthest from the actual number? Was it too high or too low? How many students gave estimates that were too high? Too low? What was the difference between the highest estimate and the lowest estimate?" Then divide the jelly beans equally and allow students to eat them.

Red, Pink, Purple, Green...
How Many Of Each Jelly Bean?

Note To The Teacher: Use with "Sorting And Graphing" on page 55.

BUNNY BUSINESS

Get a jump on springtime studies with this roundup of rabbit activities!

Real Rabbits

Get students hopping to learn about rabbits. Read *The Velveteen Rabbit* by Margery Williams (Troll Associates, 1988). Discuss what real rabbits eat and how to care for them. If possible, bring a pet rabbit to school for students to observe. Make a list of things rabbits eat, including carrot sticks. Allow children to feed carrot sticks to the rabbit. Save some for a snack!

Now "Hare" This...

There's a difference between rabbits and hares! Ask students to tell you what they know about rabbits and hares, and print that information for the students on individual index cards. Then share the following information, which you have already printed on individual index cards:

—Hares are generally larger than rabbits.
—Hares have longer ears than rabbits.
—Rabbits build nests.
—Hares do not build nests.
—Rabbits give birth to blind, helpless young.
—Hares give birth to young that are born furred and with eyes open.

Compare the similarities and differences between the two animals with a Venn diagram. Use yarn to make two large interconnecting circles on the floor. Print the words *rabbits* and *hares* on separate pieces of paper and place one at the top of each circle. Then choose an index card and read the information printed on it. Ask students to decide if the information is describing a characteristic of rabbits or hares and to place the card in the appropriate circle. If the characteristic describes both rabbits and hares, the card should be placed in the area where the circles overlap.

Hopping Down The Reading Trail

Create this bulletin board to enhance your reading program. Begin by covering a bulletin board with yellow background paper. Enlarge the rabbit pattern on page 57. Color and cut out the rabbit, and cut a slit in the basket on the dotted line indicated. Mount the rabbit on the board. Staple around the edge of the basket to create a pocket in which carrot cutouts will be placed. To make the carrots, trace several carrot shapes on orange paper and cut them out. Program each carrot with an activity that each student can complete once she's finished reading a book. Include the following activities:

—Make a poster that shows your favorite scene from the story.
—Which character was your favorite? Write a paragraph describing your favorite character.
—Read the book to another class.
—Make a diorama showing your favorite scene from the story.
—Pretend you are a character in the story. Write a letter to another character in the story describing an event that has occurred.

Place the carrots in the rabbit's basket and add the title "Hopping Down The Reading Trail." When each student has finished reading a book, encourage her to pluck a carrot from the basket. Provide students with the materials needed to complete the projects and let them hop to it!

"Wascally Wabbits"

Share the story *The Tale Of Peter Rabbit* by Beatrix Potter (Scholastic Inc., 1986). Discuss the troubles that Peter encounters. Then ask students to recall any mischief they've made—and the consequences of their mischief-making! Brainstorm and list on the board other famous rabbit rascals such as Bugs Bunny, Roger Rabbit, Bunnicula, and Harvey. Then have students write stories about these or other rabbits that make mischief. Encourage students to illustrate their stories and share them with class-mates. Display students' work on a bulletin board titled "Those Rascally Rabbits."

Bunches Of Bunnies

Math isn't a "hare-raising" experience when you tie some literature into your lessons. Share the stories *The April Rabbits* by David Cleveland (Scholastic Inc., 1986) and *Bunches And Bunches Of Bunnies* by Louise Mathews (Scholastic Inc., 1993). Both books incorporate math themes. After reading, ask students to act out simple addition, subtraction, or multiplication problems. Younger students may enjoy wearing rabbit headbands, as shown, for this activity.

Create more challenging word problems for older students such as "How many ears would be seen if eight rabbits were in a garden?" or "If six rabbits each ate four carrots, how many carrots were consumed?"

"Ears" To Math Skills!

Practice addition with a basket of bunnies! Duplicate several white bunny shapes using the pattern at the right. Cut them out. Program each of the bunny's feet with a sum; then program its body with an addition problem that corresponds to one of the sums. Program the bunny's left ear with the correct answer; then fold the ear down to cover it. Place the cutouts and a supply of cotton balls in a basket. A student chooses a bunny and solves the math problem, then places a cotton ball on his answer choice. He then checks his work by folding the bunny's ear up.

Bunny Pattern

Bunny Tail Pattern

Bodacious Bunnies

It will be difficult to keep a lid on this center that's disguised as a bunny. Use the patterns on page 60 to make several bunny and tail cutouts. Program the bunnies and tails for matching skills such as antonyms, homonyms, and synonyms. Code the backs of the cutouts with matching symbols for self-checking. Store the pieces in a large can decorated as shown to resemble a bunny. To play, students match the bunnies to the corresponding tails for bunches of basic skills practice.

Bunny Bites

Nibble on this nutritious snack of carrots and dip. To prepare bunny bites, you will need a package of carrots, eight ounces of softened cream cheese, 1/2 cup of yogurt, two tablespoons of milk, and one ten-ounce package of frozen spinach (thawed and drained). Peel and wash the carrots; then cut into bite-size pieces. Set aside. To make dip, mix together the cream cheese, milk, and yogurt. Add the spinach and combine. Place the dip in a bowl and surround with carrots. After students have helped themselves, eat and enjoy!

A "24-Carrot" Recipe

Here's a "rabbit food" recipe that's fun to prepare in the classroom! To make this salad, each student will need half of a carrot, ten raisins, five mini-marshmallows, whipped cream, a spoon, and a small cup. Bring a grater to class and assist students in grating their carrots into their cups. Mix in the raisins and minimarshmallows. Stir in the whipped cream and eat!

A BONANZA OF
BUNNY BOOKS

Rabbit's Good News
by Ruth Lercher Bornstein
(Clarion Books, 1995)

Share the story *Rabbit's Good News.* In this delightful story, Rabbit sees many signs of spring, then hops home to tell her family the news. After sharing the story, brainstorm with students the many signs of spring and list them on the board. Then instruct students to write news reports about the arrival of spring. After students have shared their reports with classmates, mount them on a board titled "Spring Has Sprung!"

Hopper Hunts For Spring
by Marcus Pfister
(North-South Books, 1992)

Share the story *Hopper Hunts For Spring* in which Hopper, a rabbit, searches for spring. What Hopper doesn't realize is that "spring" is not a person. After sharing the story, draw attention to the beautiful illustrations. Encourage students to make their own spring pictures that have the same soft effect. Each student will need a sheet of white construction paper, colored chalk, and several tissues. Instruct each student to use his chalk to draw a spring scene on his sheet of paper. After each student has finished his picture, have him use his tissues to gently rub the outlines of the drawing to create a wispy effect. Spray chalk drawings with a fixative so they don't smear.

The Rabbit's Judgment
by Suzanne Crowder Han
(Henry Holt And Company, Inc.; 1991)

Read the Korean folktale *The Rabbit's Judgment.* In the story, a tiger falls into a pit. He pleads with a man walking by to help him out. The man hesitantly agrees to do so. After the tiger is aided from the pit, he threatens to eat the man. The man is saved when a rabbit tricks the tiger into reentering the pit. After sharing the story, discuss how the clever rabbit saved the man. Then divide students into groups. Ask each group to brainstorm ways to trick the tiger into getting back into the pit. Culminate the lesson by having each group select one of its ideas to dramatize for the class.

MORE BUNNY BOOKS

- *Bunny Trouble* by Hans Wilhelm (Scholastic Inc., 1991)
- *Marshmallow* by Clare Turlay Newberry (Scholastic Inc., 1993)
- *Little Rabbit's Loose Tooth* by Lucy Bate (Crown Books For Young Readers, 1988)
- *Bunnies And Their Sports* by Nancy Carlson (Puffin Books, 1989)
- *Bunnicula: A Rabbit Tale Of Mystery* by James Howe & Deborah Howe (Atheneum Children's Book, 1979)
- *The Velveteen Rabbit* by Margery Williams (Troll Associates, 1988)

JUST HATCHED!

Spring into a season
of new birth
with these activities
about chickens and eggs.

FROM EGG TO CHICK

Welcome spring to your classroom when you incubate chicken eggs! Obtain an incubator and fertilized chicken eggs from your local agricultural extension service. After placing the eggs in the incubator, share the story *Egg To Chick* by Millicent Selsam (HarperCollins Children's Books, 1970). This book details the changes that occur inside an egg during its 21-day incubation period.

Create a classroom journal to chronicle the hatching process. Staple several large pieces of white construction paper together. Each day use Selsam's book as a reference to discuss what changes are occurring inside the eggs. Have a student volunteer dictate a sentence that will be copied into the journal. Have students illustrate the journal.

When the chicks are hatching, have your camera handy to take pictures of the special event. Place the photos in an album. Then encourage students to write news reports about the special occasion that can be read over the public-address system during the morning announcements.

LITTLE PEEPS

Create this learning center for some word-problem practice. Obtain some small pom-pom chicks (available at many craft or fabric stores). Write addition or subtraction word problems on cards, and allow students to use the chicks as math manipulatives. Or create more challenging problems for older students by adding "eggs" (minimarshmallows) to the equation. For example, how many eggs would you have if four chickens each laid five eggs? Place the cards at your math center along with the little peeps and eggs.

THE CHICKEN COOP

Students will scramble to this learning center for short-vowel-sound practice! Duplicate the chicken patterns on page 67. Color and cut out the chickens, and glue to a file folder. Laminate the folder; then use a permanent marker to program each chicken with a short vowel. Then cut out 20 eggs from white construction paper. Program each egg with a short-vowel word. Code the backs of the eggs for self-checking. To play, the student chooses an egg, reads the word, and places the egg on the correct chicken. She then turns the egg over to check her answer.

Match each egg to a chicken. Turn the egg over to check.

CHEEP OR CHEAP?

Practice homonyms with this "egg-citing" game. Trace and cut out 12 egg cutouts. Cut each egg in half, forming two puzzle pieces. Program one half of each egg with a word; program the other half with its matching homonym. To play, students set out all the egg cutouts faceup. Have students find the two matching halves for each pair of homonyms. Store the eggs in an egg carton. Vary this game by programming eggs for other matching skills such as antonyms, math facts/answers, and synonyms.

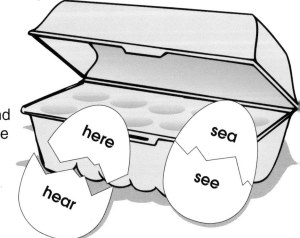

HATCH AN "EGG-CELLENT" STORY

Read the story *Seven Eggs* by Meredith Hooper (HarperCollins Publishers, 1985). Then challenge students to name animals that hatch from eggs, and list them on the board. Distribute a copy of the "Seven Sensational Eggs" reproducible on page 70, along with a pair of scissors, to each student. Have him use the student-generated list to fill in the blanks with names of animals that hatch from eggs. Cut apart the blocks of the reproducible and staple together to form a storybook. Encourage each student to illustrate his book and share it with the class.

Seven Sensational Eggs
by
Jessie

On Tuesday the second egg hatched and out came a ___robin___.

3

Sallie
She is good at math.
She is pretty.
She takes good care of our hampster.
She has a great smile.

Sallie

Kevin
He is a good runner.
He always does his homework.
He makes me laugh.
He helps me with math.

GOOD EGGS

Boost students' self-confidence with this activity. Provide each student with a large egg cutout. Instruct students to print their names on their cutouts. Collect all the eggs and then randomly distribute them to students. As soon as a student receives an egg, he reads the name on the egg and writes a positive comment about that student. After a predetermined amount of time, collect the eggs and randomly redistribute them among the students. Again each child writes a positive comment about the student on the new cutout in front of him. Repeat the process two or three more times. When the activity is over, return the eggs to their owners. Have students read the positive comments that peers wrote. Display the eggs on a bulletin board. Take an instant photo of each student to mount near his egg and personalize it. Add the title "Dozens Of Good Eggs!"

Kevin

Leanne
She is a good artist.
She doesn't talk too much in class.
She is a good reader.
She likes horses.

Bobbie
He is a good friend.
He is nice.
He is good at sports.
He has good handwriting.

Leanne

CHICKENS AREN'T THE ONLY ONES!

Share the story *Chickens Aren't The Only Ones* by Ruth Heller (Putnam Publishing Group, 1981). This story details many of the animals that reproduce by laying eggs. Challenge students to recall animals from the story that are able to lay eggs. Print these animal names on index cards. Then write the headings "fish," "amphibians," "reptiles," "birds," and "insects" on the board. As you read the animal name on each index card, have students determine in which group the animal belongs; then tape the card under that heading. Conclude the lesson by discussing the similarities among animals in a particular group.

FANCY EGGS

Share the story *Rechenka's Eggs* by Patricia Polacco (Philomel Books, 1988). In this story Babushka is saddened when her precious painted eggs are broken by an injured goose. Miraculously, the goose lays marvelously colored eggs to replace the broken ones—and she leaves behind one special egg for Babushka. Discuss with students the time it took Babushka to paint her eggs and how she felt when they were all broken.

Then let students create some beautiful eggs of their own! Each student will need a construction-paper copy of the egg pattern on page 68, colored glue, white glue, sequins, and scraps of construction paper, fabric, or ribbon. Encourage children to use the materials to decorate their construction-paper eggs. Mount the finished eggs on the board. Enlarge the goose pattern on page 69. Color and cut out the goose, and attach it to the board. Add the title "Rechenka's Eggs."

CRACK OPEN A GOOD BOOK

What's Inside? by May Garelick (Scholastic Inc., 1968)
Chester The Chick by Jane Burton (Random House, Inc.; 1988)
Here A Chick, There A Chick by Bruce McMillan (The Trumpet Club, 1983)
The Most Wonderful Egg In The World by Helme Heine (Margaret K. McElderry Books, 1983)
Little Chick's Big Day by Mary DeBall Kwitz (Scholastic Inc., 1981)

Pattern

Use with "Fancy Eggs"
on page 66.

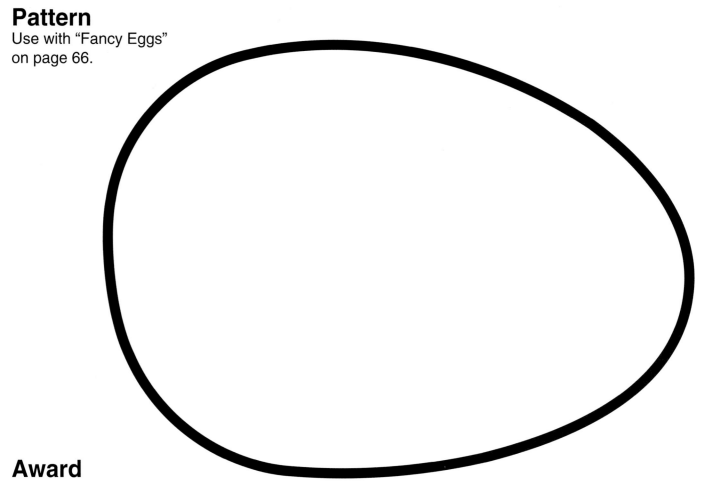

Award

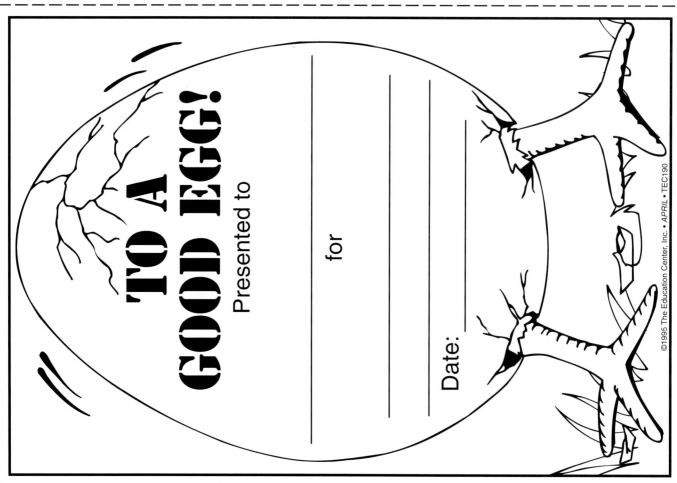

TO A GOOD EGG!

Presented to

for

Date:

©1995 The Education Center, Inc. • *APRIL* • TEC190

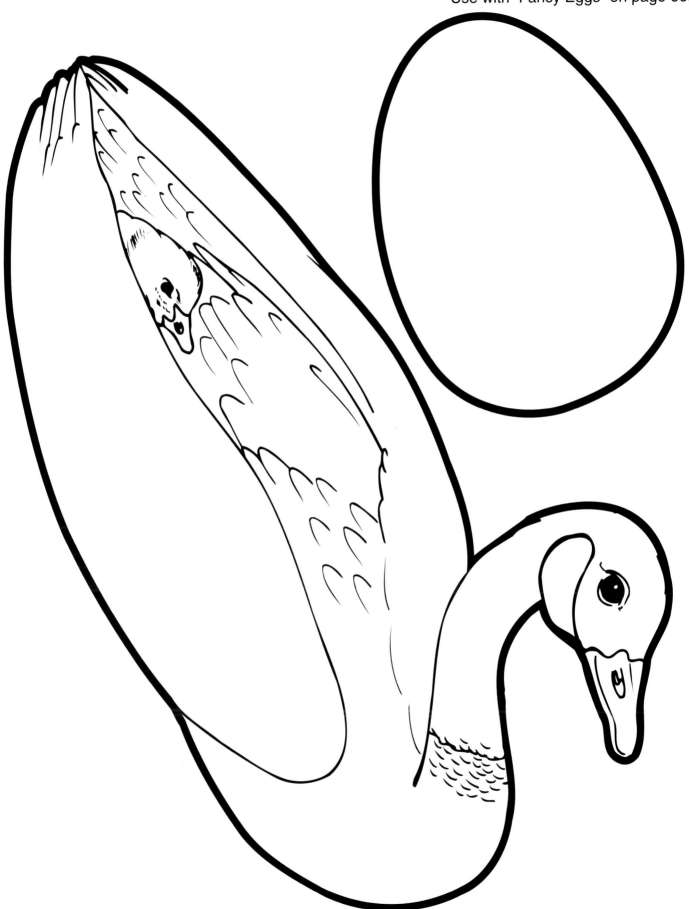

Seven Sensational Eggs

by _____

Fold here.

© 1995 The Education Center, Inc. • *APRIL* • TEC190

1

On Monday the first egg hatched and out came a _____ .

2

On Tuesday the second egg hatched and out came a _____ .

3

On Wednesday the third egg hatched and out came a _____ .

4

On Thursday the fourth egg hatched and out came a _____ .

5

On Friday the fifth egg hatched and out came a _____ .

6

On Saturday the sixth egg hatched and out came a _____ .

7

On Sunday the seventh egg hatched and out came a _____ .

Note To The Teacher: Use this reproducible with "Hatch An 'Egg-cellent' Story" on page 65.

70

©1995 The Education Center, Inc. • *APRIL* • TEC190

Let's Go To The LIBRARY!

Take note of National Library Week with this book-boosting batch of activities!
From wild imagination to worthwhile information,
your library can really "lend" a hand in learning!

Love Your Library

Create a bulletin board to display all the reasons your students love the library. Enlarge the pattern on page 76 on poster board and cut it out. Have students color the picture and mount it in the center of a bulletin board. Provide each child with a sheet of white drawing paper. Ask her to draw a picture of herself using the library and write a sentence at the bottom of the sheet describing why she enjoys going to the library. Display the students' pictures around the centerpiece. Duplicate the book pattern on page 76 on various colors of construction paper. Let each child choose a color, cut out the book pattern, and label it with her name. Add the books as a colorful border for the board. Complete the display by adding the title "Check It Out! We (heart) The Library!"

Love Your Librarian

The librarian—or media specialist—plays an important part in making the library an enjoyable place for students. Read about the librarian's job by sharing *A Day In The Life Of A Librarian* by David Paige (Troll, 1985). Then invite students to show their appreciation for your school's librarian and assistants by creating special thank-you cards. For each library worker, purchase an inexpensive card file box and a supply of small index cards to fit inside. Distribute one card to each child. Ask him to write a compliment for the recipient and draw an illustration to accompany it. Place each library worker's cards in her file box. Decorate the outside of each file box with paints, markers, or stickers. Label the boxes "Mr. [or Mrs.] _____'s Card Catalog Of Compliments." Have the students present the boxes to your librarian and assistants along with a notecard that reads as follows:

We love you for the job you do!
We love you for just being you!
You always go the extra mile,
So choose a card to make you smile!

Guess Who!

Invite students to come to school one day dressed as their favorite book characters. Ask each student to write a brief description about the identity of her character, the book or books in which her character appears, and why she chose the character. Let students present their characters to the class, then join in a book-character parade through your school to share their costumes with other classes and staff. Then photograph each child in her costume and place the photos in an album, along with the child's description written on an index card. Keep the album in the library for students to enjoy.

On The Title Trail

Give your students practice with using the library and its resources by conducting a library scavenger hunt. Program page 75 with the authors, subjects, and titles of your choice (depending on your class's interests and abilities). Then duplicate the page for each of your students to fill in. Set up a convenient time with your school media specialist for your class to conduct their hunt. Then set a time limit and discuss your rules for the event. Award prizes to all who successfully complete the search.

It's In The Bag!

Your students will want to "check out" these book reports! Ask each student to borrow a book from the library and prepare a paper-bag book report to share with the class. Provide each student with a large paper grocery bag. Have him decorate the outside of the bag with pictures that tell something about the story he read. He should also print the title and author of his book on the outside of the bag. Then he must find some small objects to place inside the bag that represent the story, its setting, or its characters. Have each child present his report, withdrawing items from the bag and telling why he chose each one. Display a few of the paper-bag reports in the library each week to spark students' interest in new books.

A Center That's Long Overdue

Create this math learning center to give students practice with calendar skills. Provide an outdated calendar page or a copy of a calendar for any month. Make up a series of word problems similar to those listed below. Tailor the questions for use with your particular calendar. Print the problems on numbered index cards. Place the cards, the calendar, and a supply of blank paper in a large string-tie envelope for students to use independently. Each child should write his name on a blank piece of paper, choose a card, and solve the problem using the calendar. He can write the card numbers and his answers on his paper.

Door Decor

Get your whole school involved in celebrating Library Week with a door-decorating contest. Have each class decorate their door to resemble a favorite book cover or illustration. Have your school principal, media specialist, and PTA president act as a panel of judges. Treat the winning class to a special storytime at the library and a gift certificate (donated by a local bookstore) to purchase books for a classroom library.

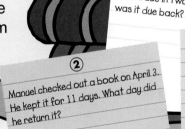

APRIL

	1	2	3	4	5	6
7	8	9	17	11	12	13
14	15	16		18	19	20
21	22	23	24	25	26	27
28	29	30				

① Tai checked out a book on the 9th. It was due in two weeks. What day was it due back?

② Manuel checked out a book on April 3. He kept it for 11 days. What day did he return it?

③ Jamie checked out a new book on each Tuesday in April. How many books did she check out during the whole month?

Bookworm Buddies

Do your students have difficulty keeping up with traditional bookmarks that slide down or fall out of picture books? Then they'll love creating these wriggly page pals. Provide each student with a 9" x 2" strip of green construction paper. Have the student fold the paper in half and draw the squiggly outline of a worm as shown. Have him cut out the worm shape and draw a face with fine-tip markers. (You can laminate the bookmarks at this point, if desired.) Give each student two small squares of magnetic tape and have him attach the pieces at the inside bottom of the bookmark as shown. Now the bookworm is ready to wiggle down between the pages of your library book. The magnets will attract to keep this pal in the right place!

magnetic tape

Little Red

LIBRARY LITERATURE

Lots of books are in the library, but these books are about the library!

I Took My Frog To The Library
by Eric A. Kimmel
(Puffin Books, 1990)

Your students will enjoy this funny story about the unacceptable behavior of pets at the library. After sharing it with your class, invite students to write a class innovation. Have each child choose an animal, and complete this sentence at the bottom of a sheet of white drawing paper:

I took my <u>duck</u> to the library, but <u>he went swimming in the water fountain</u>.

After students illustrate their sentences, bind the pages together in a book for your class library.

The Library Dragon
by Carmen A. Deedy
(Peachtree Publishers,Ltd.; 1994)

Imagine a school librarian who's a real dragon—literally! Miss Lotta Scales guards the library books fiercely until she is tamed by a near-sighted dragon-slayer. Carmen Deedy uses a multitude of plays on words in this book, all associated with dragons and fire. Review the text with students and challenge them to list all the dragon-related vocabulary words.

How A Book Is Made
by Aliki
(Thomas Y. Crowell, 1986)

Your students will be amazed to discover the people, time, and effort involved in producing a printed book. The illustrations in this book are small, so try sharing it with small groups of students. After reading the book, ask students to search for clues throughout the book as to how long it took from the date when the author began writing to the time when the book was purchased from the store.

Aunt Lulu
by Daniel Pinkwater
(Macmillan Publishing Company, 1988)

Aunt Lulu is a librarian in Alaska who delivers books on a dogsled! Then she moves to Parsippany, New Jersey, with all 14 of her huskies in tow. Ask students to imagine holding the job of librarian in an unusual setting, such as on a tropical island or out in space. What are some ways to transport books? Who would read the borrowed books? Invite students to do some creative writing about a librarian in an unusual location.

LOOK IT UP AT THE LIBRARY!

1. Find one book by each of the following authors. Write the title on the blank line.

AUTHOR   TITLE

A. _____   _____

B. _____   _____

C. _____   _____

D. _____   _____

E. _____   _____

2. Look up _____ in the encyclopedia.
   (subject)

   Which volume is it in? _____

3. Use the card catalog to look up _____.
   (subject)

   How many books are listed? _____

4. Use the card catalog to look up _____.
   (title)

   What's the reference number for this book? _____

5. Find a book about _____.
   (subject)

   List the title and the author. _____

   _____

6. Find two magazines. List their names.

   _____

   _____

Note To The Teacher: Use with "On The Title Trail" on page 72.

Patterns

Use with "Love Your Library" on page 71.

Take Me Out To The Ball Game!

When spring fever strikes, take a swing at these baseball activities and score some home runs with your students!

Hometown Home-Run Heroes

Introduce students to America's national pastime with a visit from a local baseball hero. Contact a local team and invite a professional player to come dressed in his uniform and speak to the class. Before his arrival, ask students to think of appropriate questions to ask him. Find out whom his favorite baseball heroes are!

Display the list of baseball heroes below. Have students add their favorite players to the list. Let older students work with a partner to find out all about one of these baseball players. For an oral presentation, have one student dress as the player and stand before the class. His partner, acting as a news reporter, asks him questions about his life. Which players were named Players Of The Year? Which ones are in the Baseball Hall Of Fame?

Hank Aaron; Johnny Bench; Roberto Clemente; Ty Cobb; Joe DiMaggio; Lou Gehrig; Reggie Jackson; Sandy Koufax; Mickey Mantle; Roger Maris; Don Mattingly; Willie Mays; Stan Musial; Satchel Paige; Pee Wee Reese; Cal Ripken, Jr.; Phil Rizzuto; Jackie Robinson; Babe Ruth; Nolan Ryan; Duke Snider; Casey Stengel; Fernando Valenzuela; Ted Williams; Carl Yastrzemski

Baseball Bookmarks

Encourage reading with these baseball incentives. Duplicate the baseball bookmark on page 84 on red construction paper for each child. When each student completes a book, use a hole puncher to punch out a baseball on his bookmark. When all of the baseballs are punched out, reward the student with a pack of baseball cards. See the "Baseball Book List" on page 85 to get your rookie readers started.

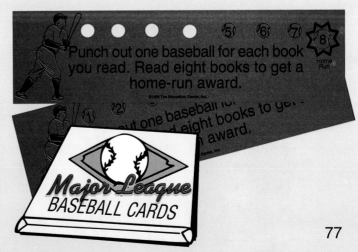

Punch out one baseball for each book you read. Read eight books to get a home-run award.

Major League BASEBALL CARDS

Baseball Card Superstars

Collecting baseball cards is a hobby for millions of people of all ages. It is also a billion-dollar business. In the early 1880s, cards with the baseball players' pictures and last names came in packages of tobacco. After World War I, candy companies began including baseball cards in packages of toffee, caramels, and mints. Baseball cards with the players' photos on the front and vital statistics on the back were introduced in bubble-gum packages in the 1930s. Today five major companies produce seven sets of collectors' cards each year.

Have students create their own baseball cards for a classroom display. Bring in a pack of cards purchased at your local drugstore. Allow students to handle and examine the cards and discuss the biographical information included on the backs. Then, for a fun twist, ask each student to design an oversized baseball card about himself. Have the student draw a picture of himself on one side of a 9" x 12" piece of unlined paper and add his name. On the back each child writes information about himself as shown. Laminate your students' cards and display them with the title "Mrs. _____'s Classroom Heroes."

Bobby Fletcher

Hometown:
Raleigh, NC
Family: Mom, Dad, 1 brother, 1 sister
Favorite Sport:
basketball
Future Plans:
to be a veterinarian

Hometown:
Columbus, OH
Family: Mom, Dad, 1 brother, and my cat, Percy
Favorite Sport:
bike riding
Future Plans:
to be the first lady President of the United States

Zach Williams

Hometown:
Dallas, TX
Family: Mom, Dad, 2 brothers, and 1 sister
Favorite Sport:
football
Future Plans:
to be a coach for a pro football team or a sports announcer

Kristie Allen

The Baseball Hall Of Fame

The National Baseball Hall Of Fame And Museum is located in Cooperstown, New York. Founded in 1939, the museum immortalizes baseball's greatest players. In most cases, candidates for this honor must have been retired at least five years and have played ten years or more in the major leagues. Which players, past or present, would your students like to place in the Baseball Hall Of Fame?

To find out, create a Baseball Hall Of Fame bulletin board to encourage research and creative writing. Make two copies of a baseball pattern for each student. Have each student write a player's name on one baseball and write why the player is a hero on the other baseball (the student must include facts to support his reasons). The student cuts out the balls and staples them together as shown. Display the baseballs on a bulletin board with a string of student-made baseball pennants and the title "Our Baseball Hall Of Fame." Let students lift the flaps to discover baseball facts.

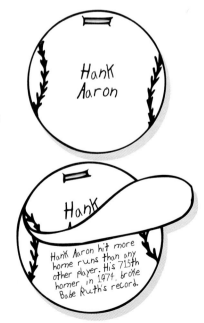

Hank Aaron

Hank

Hank Aaron hit more home runs than any other player. His 715th homer, in 1974, broke Babe Ruth's record.

Take A Swing At These!

Challenge student teams to take a swing at these baseball questions to practice using reference materials. Enlarge, color, and cut out the baseball pitcher on page 88. Cut out and program each of 15 baseballs with one of the questions at the right. Mount the baseballs on a bulletin board along with the pitcher. Add the title "Take A Swing At These!" Provide resources such as sports trivia books, almanacs, atlases, newspaper and magazine articles, encyclopedias, and dictionaries for students to use in their research. Divide students into teams to discover the answers together. Provide a record sheet for each team to write its answers on, as well as the resource titles and page numbers where the answers were found. Teams score one run for choosing the correct kind of reference book and one run for each correct answer. Together students will score some runs for research!

—What is a batter doing if he is pinch-hitting?
—How many players are in the outfield?
—Where is the dugout?
—Who is a southpaw?
—Why would a batter bunt?
—What is the seventh-inning stretch?
—Where is the Baseball Hall Of Fame?
—Where is Candlestick Park?
—How fast is a fastball?
—When does a batter walk to first base?
—What is a rookie?
—What does a shortstop do?
—What is an MVP?
—What does RBI mean?
—Where is spring training held?

Baseball Bingo

Play Baseball Bingo to increase spelling and vocabulary skills. Duplicate the baseball vocabulary word cards on page 86 for each child and make two copies for yourself. Save one copy and cut your other copy apart. Place the cards in a baseball cap. Make a bingo card for each student as shown. Have each student fill in each block with a different word from his vocabulary sheet.

Provide popcorn for students to use as markers. Pull a card from the hat and call out the word. Players who have that word on their cards cover it with popcorn. Play continues until one student covers five words in a row (across or down) and calls out, "Baseball!" To vary, read the definitions on the word cards and have students find each word you are defining.

southpaw–a left-handed pitcher

infield–area inside the baselines

Play Ball!

Pass the baseball cap for vocabulary review. Write the definitions of the baseball words on page 86 on index cards and place them in a baseball cap. Pass the cap around a circle of six students and have each student—in turn—pick a card, read it aloud, and guess the vocabulary word. Each time a student is correct, she scores a point. Keep track of the scores on the board. If a student answers incorrectly, she simply places the card back in the hat and passes it to the next child.

Little League Lineup

Little League baseball was started in 1939 in Williamsport, Pennsylvania, with three teams of boys. By 1994 Little League baseball was played in 81 countries all over the world. More than 2.8 million boys and girls aged 5 to 18 played on 190,000 teams!

Have students create their own Little League lineup to encourage creative thinking and to practice alphabetizing. Ask your students if they play on or know of any local Little League teams. Write the names of the teams on sentence strips. Help students arrange the strips in ABC order.

Then divide students into groups and have each group decide on a team name for itself. Provide each group with an enlarged copy of the T-shirt pattern on page 87. Have groups design their own team T-shirts. Students cut out and clip the T-shirts in ABC order onto a clothesline for an alphabetical Little League lineup.

If I were a baseball, I would fly fast and far out of the ballpark. Up high in the sky, over my house, and out of town I'd fly!

Ryan

If I Were A Baseball...

Hit some home runs for creative writing. Ask each child to imagine what it would be like to be a baseball hit high into the sky. Would she sail out of the stadium and around the world? Would she linger high above the ballpark or zoom into the crowd? Or would she want to be bunted low, roll around, and hide in the dust? Would she head for her favorite outfielder's glove or elude the whole team? Have each student write and illustrate a story from the point of view of an adventurous baseball. Students will love sharing their adventures and thinking up new tales to top the ones they've heard!

Baseball Buddies

Everyone should have a Baseball Buddy to encourage good behavior. Have each child trace and cut out an eight-inch circle from a piece of white construction paper for the Baseball Buddy's head. Cut out two hands and two athletic shoes from the scraps. Have each student draw stitching and a face on her circle, as shown, with a black marker or crayon. Provide red yarn and large, blunt, plastic needles so students can stitch along the dotted lines on the baseball heads if desired.

Provide each student with two 2" x 12" strips of colored construction paper (legs) and two 2" x 8" strips of colored construction paper (arms). Demonstrate how to accordion-fold the strips. Glue the hands and shoes to the ends of the strips. Then attach the arms and legs to the baseball head as shown. Provide colored paper to students so they can draw, cut out, and glue on personalized hats to complete their Baseball Buddies. Each day that a student exhibits good behavior, give her a gummed gold star to stick on her Baseball Buddy's cap. You're sure to have some all-star players each week!

Here's The Pitch For Math Measurement!

Provide students with the facts below, several sizes of bats, an assortment of balls, and measuring tapes. Have students complete the activities that accompany the facts.

—A baseball has a cork-and-rubber center wrapped tightly with yarn and covered with leather. It weighs five ounces and is nine inches around. Compare the baseball's circumference to those of other balls.

—A big-league regulation bat is made of hardwood and cannot be longer than 42 inches. Little League bats cannot be longer than 33 inches. Estimate the lengths of several bats. Then, measure each and place them in order by length. Measure distances in "bat units."

—The distance between the bases is 90 feet in the major leagues, but only 60 feet in Little League. Measure these distances on the playground.

Catcher's Mitt Math

Students will catch on to math facts with a pocketful of balls. Make six copies of the catcher's mitt pattern on page 88 on tan construction paper. Make 24 copies of the baseball pattern on page 88 on white construction paper. Program the balls with math facts and the mitts with corresponding answers. Laminate and cut out the mitts and balls; then use a permanent marker to program the back of each mitt with an answer key.

Place the pieces in a string-tie envelope. A student lays out the mitts, chooses a ball, and places it on the correct mitt. When all balls are placed, the student turns each mitt over to check the answer key.

Batting A Thousand

Provide your players with big-league practice in math. Bring in the sports page of your local newspaper, and have student pairs write addition or subtraction word problems based on the baseball scores. Each pair writes a word problem on a baseball cutout, trades balls with another pair, and solves the problem. Continue until all balls have been traded and students are batting a thousand!

He's Safe!

An early form of baseball called *rounders* was played in New England in the early 1700s. The rules of the game allowed players to throw the ball at the runner. If he was hit, he was out. Ouch! This was called *soaking* or *plugging* the runners. In the 1830s or '40s, players began tagging the runners out.

Prepare for a discussion of how baseball rules, uniforms, and equipment have changed for safety's sake. Display photos of baseball players from the past. Provide examples of the latest in bats, balls, mitts, gloves, and protective helmets for students to examine. Bring in old, outdated equipment for comparison. Have students research and list five ways that the rules and equipment of baseball have evolved to make the game safer.

Spring Training Camp

It's spring training time—time to get baseball players into playing shape! Conduct your own spring training camp on the playground and have students pair up for some fitness fun.

Give each student pair a clipboard, a pencil, and a list of exercises: ten toe touches, ten hands-on-hips waist bends, ten jumping jacks, ten lunges to the left, ten lunges to the right, ten deep knee bends, ten sit-ups with knees bent, ten push-ups. Partners check each other as they complete their preseason warm-ups each day. Then play ball!

toe touches ✔
waist bends ✔
jumping jacks ✔
lunges to left ✔
lunges to right ✔
deep knee bends ✔
sit-ups ✔
push-ups ✔

The Seventh-Inning Stretch

It's the end of the sixth inning. Before the next team comes to bat at the top of the seventh, all the fans in the stadium stand and stretch. Ask students how they think this tradition, called the *seventh-inning stretch*, got started. No one knows the answer, but if your students have been sitting for a long time, they too may welcome some stretching exercises. Have students stand beside their desks and do some deep knee bends and toe touches to a recorded version of "Take Me Out To The Ball Game." Teach the lyrics to the song and then surprise students with a snack of Cracker Jack® glazed popcorn and peanuts! Your baseball fans will be reenergized and ready to learn!

All-Star Players

You can recognize all the players in your room who are making progress in any subject. Label a chart for each subject area using some of the sample titles below, and add student names to the rosters for achievements or improvement. Duplicate the award on page 87 for individual progress and team effort.

Spelling Sluggers
Rookie Readers
Mighty Math Stars
Big-League Writers
World Series Of Science

You're A
Big-League Player!
Grant Rogers
hit a home run in
addition and
subtraction
Teacher: Ms. Jones Date: 4/7/96

Major-League Geography

Explain to students that professional baseball players get paid to play ball. Players begin in the minor leagues, and the best ones move up to big salaries in the major leagues. There are 26 major-league teams in the United States and 2 in Canada. Teams travel across the country to play each other in the eastern, central, and western divisions of the American and National Leagues. The top team from each league plays in the World Series. This best-of-seven series of games has been played every year since 1903, except for 1904 and 1994.

Provide a large map of the United States and Canada, and have students locate these hometown teams. For some additional learning, have students put the teams in ABC order.

American League

Eastern Division	Central Division	Western Division
New York Yankees	Chicago White Sox	Texas Rangers
Baltimore Orioles	Cleveland Indians	Oakland Athletics
Toronto Blue Jays	Kansas City Royals	Seattle Mariners
Boston Red Sox	Minnesota Twins	California Angels
Detroit Tigers	Milwaukee Brewers	

National League

Eastern Division	Central Division	Western Division
Montreal Expos	Cincinnati Reds	Los Angeles Dodgers
Atlanta Braves	Houston Astros	San Francisco Giants
New York Mets	Pittsburgh Pirates	Colorado Rockies
Philadelphia Phillies	St. Louis Cardinals	San Diego Padres
Florida Marlins	Chicago Cubs	

Baseball Bookmark

Use with "Baseball Bookmarks" on page 77.

① ② ③ ④ ⑤ ⑥ ⑦ ⑧ Home Run

Punch out one baseball for each book you read. Read eight books to get a home-run award.

① ② ③ ④ ⑤ ⑥ ⑦ ⑧ Home Run

Punch out one baseball for each book you read. Read eight books to get a home-run award.

Rookie Reading Corner

Decorate a corner of your room with baseball memorabilia—pennants, hats, shirts, collectible figures, autographed baseballs, baseball cards, and posters. Provide books about baseball in a gym bag beside a comfy beanbag chair for some home-run reading.

Hooray For Snail!
by John Stadler
(HarperCollins Children's Books, 1984)

Young students will cheer as this happy snail makes his way around the bases. There's plenty of time for Snail to score. His baseball bounces all over the earth and even into outer space before it is caught.

After sharing this early-reader story, have students illustrate in sequence the places Snail's ball bounced.

Teammates
by Peter Golenbock
(HarBrace Juvenile Books, 1992)

Friendship is the theme of this story about Jackie Robinson. With the support of a teammate, Jackie Robinson withstood the pressures of being the first black player in major-league baseball.

After reading the book aloud, discuss the courageous actions of Jackie Robinson's teammate, Pee Wee Reese. Ask each student to think of a time when she stood up for a friend. Encourage students to talk about times when being a friend is not easy.

To remind students of this lesson, teach them to make friendship bracelets. You will need a six-inch piece of yarn or leather cord and a variety of colorful beads for each child. These are available at a craft or hobby store. Each student strings beads onto her piece of yarn and ties it around her wrist. Students will want to wear their bracelets every day to remind them of what being a good friend really means.

Ronald Morgan Goes To Bat
by Patricia R. Giff
(Puffin Books, 1990)

Ronald Morgan loves baseball. Although he can't hit, run, or catch well, he's got team spirit! When it comes to sportsmanship and perseverance, Ronald is a winner.

After reading, discuss how some teammates were negative and how some encouraged Ronald. Discuss how students can encourage each other. You'll have classmates cheering each other on—not because they are recognized for doing so, but because it makes others feel good and it's the right thing to do.

Baseball Book List

The Lucky Baseball Bat by Matt Christopher (Little, Brown And Company; 1993)
The Hit-Away Kid by Matt Christopher (Little, Brown And Company; 1990)
Skinnybones by Barbara Park (Alfred A. Knopf Books For Young Readers, 1982)

Baseball Vocabulary Word Cards

bunt—a ball that is not hit with a full swing of the bat

fastball—the fastest ball a pitcher can throw; a high hard ball

inning—both teams have a turn at bat, ending with three outs for each team

pinch hitter—a batter who takes the place of another batter in a pinch (when a hit is badly needed)

shortstop—the infield player position between the second and third bases

windup—a pitching position involving the winding or swinging of the arm before letting the ball go

bullpen—the area next to the foul lines where pitchers warm up

error—a mistake made by a player that allows a runner to move to the next base

infield—the area inside the baselines

outfield—the area beyond the baselines bordered by the fence or stands

seventh-inning stretch—when fans stand up, stretch, and show support for their teams before the seventh inning

strikeout—when a batter is charged with three strikes and sent back to the dugout

batboy/batgirl—a boy or girl hired to handle the bats and care for the equipment

dugout—an area with a long bench where the players sit

home plate—a five-sided slab of white rubber (A runner must reach the plate to score a run.)

mound—the small hill where the pitcher stands

safe—when the umpire declares that the runner reached the base or home plate before the ball did

steal—when a runner runs to the next base without benefit of a base hit; a stolen base

bases—white canvas bags that a runner must touch on his way to home plate

diamond—the infield of the baseball field, inside the baselines

foul ball—any batted ball that lands out-of-bounds

line drive—a ball that is hit hard and travels straight and low

rookie—a first-year player

spitball—an illegal pitch made by wetting the ball with spit or sweat, causing it to sink in midair

amateur—a player who plays for fun and does not get paid

catcher—the fielder who squats behind the plate to catch the pitch

fly-out—a fair ball that is caught before it touches the ground

knuckleball—a wild pitch thrown by holding the ball with the fingertips or knuckles

pop fly—a pop-up ball hit high into the air and easily caught

southpaw—a left-handed pitcher

Note To The Teacher: Use with "Baseball Bingo" and "Play Ball!" on page 80.

You're A Big-League Player!

_____

(student)

hit a home run in

_____

_____ !

Teacher: _____ Date: _____

©1995 The Education Center, Inc. • *APRIL* • TEC190

T-shirt Pattern
Use with "Little League Lineup"
on page 80.

Patterns

Use the pitcher pattern with "Take A Swing At These!" on page 79
and the catcher's mitt and baseball patterns with "Catcher's Mitt Math" on page 82.

Fine-Feathered Friends

This flock of fun ideas is guaranteed to make bird lovers out of you and your students.

Bird Lovers Unite!

Begin your bird unit by sharing the story *She's Wearing A Dead Bird On Her Head!* by Kathryn Lasky (Hyperion Books For Children, 1995). This story details how one of the first chapters of the Audubon Society began. Harriet Hemenway and Minna Hall, two Boston women, decided to start a bird-protection club when they noticed women wearing dead birds on their hats for decorations.

After reading the story, ask students, "How many of you have ever heard of the Audubon Society? What do people in the Audubon Society try to do?" Display some bird drawings by John James Audubon. Explain that the Audubon Society is named for John James Audubon—a naturalist who is known for his drawings of birds in their natural habitats and a publisher of several books about birds.

Bird Feeder Fun

Give your budding naturalists a chance to view birds close-up with their own feather-friendly bird feeders. Provide each student with a piece of waxed paper, a rice cake, peanut butter, a plastic knife, birdseed, and string. Have each student place his rice cake on his waxed paper. Spread peanut butter on both sides of the rice cake; then sprinkle birdseed over the peanut butter. Use a nutpick to make a hole in the rice cake; then tie a length of string through the hole. Have each student take his feeder home in a plastic baggie and suspend it from a branch. Don't forget to make a couple of extra feeders to attract birds to your schoolyard.

Bird-Watchers At Work

Encourage students to do some bird-watching at home. Provide each student with a copy of the "Bird-Watchers At Work" chart on page 95. When the chart is complete, have the student bring it to school. Allow students to cut out the Bird-Watcher Badge and wear proudly.

Challenge each student to draw, color, and cut out pictures of birds that are observed at home. When each student returns a bird cutout, allow him to tape it to a large chart titled "Birds We've Seen." Provide several reference books, such as *Crinkleroot's Guide To Knowing The Birds* by Jim Arnosky (Bradbury Press, 1992) and *Families Of Birds* by Oliver L. Austin, Jr. (Western Publishing Company, Inc.; 1971), so that students can label the birds. To culminate your unit, take a field trip to a bird sanctuary or a nature center. Many provide guided tours for school-age children.

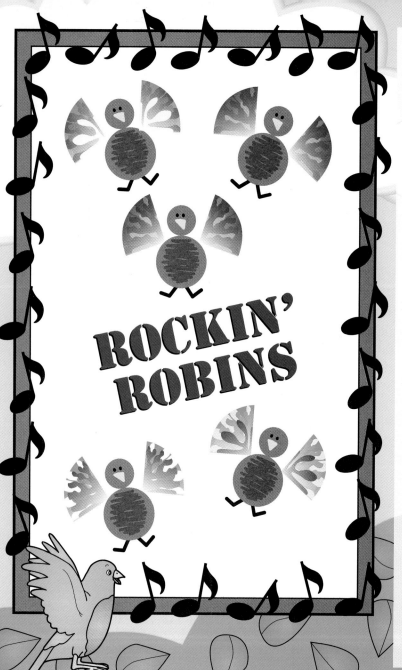

Rockin' Robins

Spring into fun with these student-made robins. To make a robin, each student will need 1/2 of a small coffee filter, a two-inch circle, a three-inch circle, nonpermanent markers, a small cup of water, a piece of waxed paper, one six-inch piece of pipe cleaner, scissors, glue, two wiggle eyes, and tape. Have each student use her markers to color the coffee filter. Then have each student fold the filter in half three times so that it resembles a pie slice. Next instruct each student to place the tip of the filter into the cup of water so that the colors from the markers spread. Have each student place her filter on the waxed paper to dry.

While the filters are drying, have each student color her circles to represent the head and body of the bird. Glue the smaller circle to the larger circle; then glue on the wiggle eyes. Form the legs by cutting the pipe cleaner in half. Tape the resulting pieces to the back of the bird's body. When the filter is dry, have each student cut her filter in two. Have each student glue the resulting pieces to either side of the bird's body for wings. Mount the birds on a bulletin board. Add a border of musical notes and the title "Rockin' Robins."

Whirling, Twirling Birds

These beautiful birds blow in the breeze. To make a whirly bird, each student will need scissors, a length of string, markers, glue, four 12" streamers or ribbons, one 1 1/2" x 11" construction-paper strip, one 1 1/2" x 9" construction-paper strip, and one 1 1/2" x 8" construction-paper strip. Instruct each student to color the strips, then make a head for his bird by gluing his 9" strip into a loop. To make a body for the bird, repeat the process with the 11" strip. Make small cuts on both ends of the 8" strip to create feathers. Glue the 8" strip to the body; then glue the head to the top of the body as shown. Then add eyes and a construction-paper beak. Next glue the streamers or ribbons to the back of the bird's body, forming a tail. Tie a length of string through each bird's head and suspend the birds near a classroom window to catch a breeze.

Chirping Birds

These sweet-sounding birds will bring music to your ears. To make a chirping bird, each student will need a yellow plastic cup, scissors, a small square of orange construction paper, two craft feathers, a one-inch piece of sponge, string, glue, and a felt-tip marker.

Instruct each student to turn his cup upside down; then have him use a felt-tip marker to draw eyes on the cup. Have each student cut a beak from his orange paper and glue it to the cup as shown. Instruct each student to glue the feathers to the back of the cup. Next have each student thread his length of string through the piece of sponge. Use scissors to carefully poke a hole through the cup as shown and thread the string through, knotting it to hang. Dampen the sponge and move it up and down the string to hear a "tweet" sound.

Nibble Nests

Let students nibble on these edible nests. To make 24 nests, you'll need 8 large shredded-wheat biscuits, 1 cup of coconut, 4 tablespoons of brown sugar, 1 cup of margarine (melted), 2 bags of jelly beans, and muffin tins with a total of 24 muffin cups that have been lined with foil.

Crumble the shredded wheat in a bowl and stir in the coconut, sugar, and melted margarine. Press the resulting mixture into each of the 24 foil-lined muffin cups. Bake at 350 degrees for 10 minutes. When the nests have cooled, remove them from the foil-lined muffin cups and fill with jelly beans. Allow students to eat the snacks while you read *A First Look At Birds' Nest* by Millicent Selsam (Walker & Co., 1984).

Eat Like A Bird

Students will enjoy nibbling on this "tweet" treat that they have helped prepare. In advance ask each student to bring in a plastic bag filled with 100 tiny treats such as raisins, sunflower seeds, popcorn, minimarshmallows, peanuts, or cereal. To make the treat, dump each student's contribution into a large mixing bowl. Scoop out a cupful of the tasty treat for each student to enjoy.

While students are eating their snacks, engage them in a math activity. Tape a graph to the board that is similar to the one shown. Have each student name the type of treat he brought in, and have him fill in an appropriate space on the graph. When the graph is complete, ask students to solve word problems using the information on the chart.

Let's All Eat Like Birds!
Predict what snack we'll have the most of:

Number Of Students (13 12 11 10 9 8 7 6 5 4 3 2 1)

Snacks: raisins, peanuts, mini-marshmallows, popcorn, pretzels, Cheerios®, sunflower seeds, chocolate chips, other

Tangram Birds

Try these terrific tangram teasers. To begin this math activity, provide each student with a copy of the tangram pattern. Instruct each student to cut out his tangram pieces and, working atop a sheet of white paper, use them to form a bird shape. When each student has completed his tangram bird, instruct him to trace around his shape. Have each student remove his tangram pieces and set them next to his white paper.

Then have students take a tangram tour. Instruct each student to move to another student's desk and look at the outline drawn on the white paper. Each student attempts to reproduce the shape using the tangram pieces next to the outline. Repeat this process two or three more times. Conclude the lesson by having students make up names for the birds they created with the tangram pieces.

Tangram Pattern

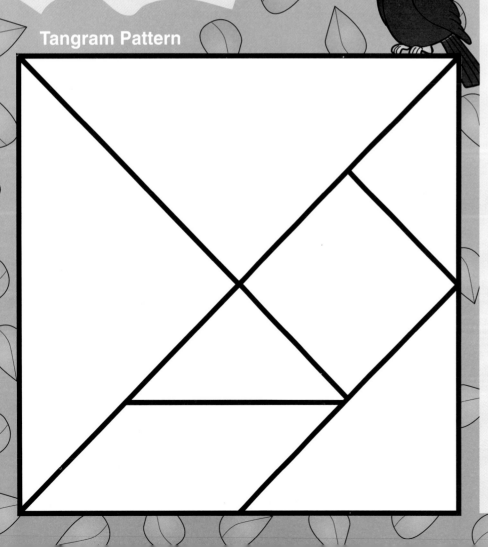

Birdbrained Legends

Birds are featured in many fables and native legends. Share some of these stories with your class: *Raven: A Trickster Tale From The Pacific Northwest* by Gerald McDermott (HarBrace Juvenile Books, 1993), *The Loon's Necklace* by Elizabeth Cleaver (Oxford University Press, Inc.; 1990), *How The Guinea Fowl Got Her Spots* by Barbara Knutson (Carolrhoda Books, Inc.; 1991) and *Owl Eyes* by Frieda Gates (Lothrop, Lee & Shepard Books; 1994). After sharing the stories, complete a chart to compare the settings, characters, and the roles of the birds in each story.

Then challenge students to write their own bird tales. Have students brainstorm their own topics for stories and list them on the board. Students may come up with ideas such as "How The Toucan Got Its Colors," "Why The Owl Sleeps All Day," "Why The Robin Has A Red Breast," or "Why The Ostrich Can't Fly." When each student has finished her story, allow her to share it with the class. Bind students' stories into a classroom collection called "Birds Of A Feather Flock Together."

Something To Chirp About

Create this file folder for some extra vowel practice. Enlarge the robin pattern; then duplicate it five times. Color and cut out the robins; then glue them to a file folder. Program each of the robins with a vowel. Next cut 20 worm shapes from beige paper. Program each of the worms with a short-vowel word. Code the back for self-checking. Put the worms in a resealable plastic bag and clip to the file folder. Place the game at a center. To play, students choose a worm, read the word printed on it, then place the worm on the appropriate robin.

Robin Pattern

Good Books To Chirp About

The Best Beak In Boonaroo Bay
by Narelle Oliver
(Fulcrum, 1995)

Share the story *The Best Beak In Boonaroo Bay* with students. In this story Spoonbill, Darter, Cormorant, Oyster-Catcher, and Curlew argue incessantly over who has the most exquisite beak. Finally the wise Pelican tells the birds to have a contest to determine who has the best beak. During the contest the birds participate in five events, and they begin to realize that each of their beaks is different and designed for a special purpose.

After reading, discuss the different shapes of the birds' beaks and the jobs that they can do. Remind students that the shape of a bird's bill reflects its use. For example, the hooked bills of birds of prey are used to kill and tear the small animals they feed on. The bills of waterfowl are adapted for feeding on a variety of plants, small fish, insects, and shellfish. Some birds that live along the shoreline have long thin beaks that are ideal for reaching animals, like shellfish, that live beneath the sand. Seed-eating birds have beaks that can vary a great deal. Some have small beaks suited to the tiny seeds they eat; others have strong beaks and powerful jaws that can crush their food.

Finally engage students in this "beaks-on" activity to help them understand the uses of different beaks. Provide an array of utensils such as two spoons, a pair of tongs, and a nutcracker to represent different birds' bills. Challenge students to try doing various tasks with each utensil, such as picking up insects (pieces of cereal) or cracking seeds (walnuts). After each student has had a turn, compare and contrast the ease or difficulty of using each utensil for a particular task.

Tico And The Golden Wings
by Leo Lionni
(Alfred A. Knopf Books For
Young Readers, 1975)

Share the story *Tico And The Golden Wings*. This delightful story tells how a little bird uses his golden wings to make others happy. After sharing the story, ask students to think about how they can make people feel happy. Cut out a feather from gold-colored foil for each student. Instruct each student to write on her feather a way to make people happy. Staple the feathers around a bird cutout to make a large golden bird. Add the title "Our Bird Of Happiness."

Are You My Mother?
by Philip D. Eastman
(Random House Books For
Young Readers, 1986)

Share the story *Are You My Mother?* This story tells of a baby bird who enters the world while his mother is away from the nest. The baby bird searches for her, and along the way he meets many animate and inanimate objects. To each he asks, "Are you my mother?" Finally the baby bird meets a large steam shovel that moves while he is perched upon it. The bird is deposited by the steam shovel into his nest just as his mother arrives.

After sharing the story, allow students to act out this tale. Select one student to be the baby bird and assign other students the remaining roles. If desired, change or add to the story by brainstorming other animals or objects that the bird can ask, "Are you my mother?"

Name _____

Bird observation

I'm Feather Friendly!

TEC190

Bird-Watchers At Work!

I predict that I will see _____ birds.

What color was the bird?	What size and shape was the bird?	What sounds did the bird make?	What other details did you observe?	What bird do you think it is? Why?

Note To The Teacher: Use with "Bird-Watchers At Work" on page 89.

Name _____

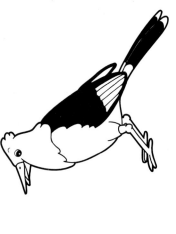

Our Fine-Feathered Friends

Four bird pictures are missing!
Read the clues below each box.
Then cut and paste the missing bird names.
In each box, draw and color the missing bird.

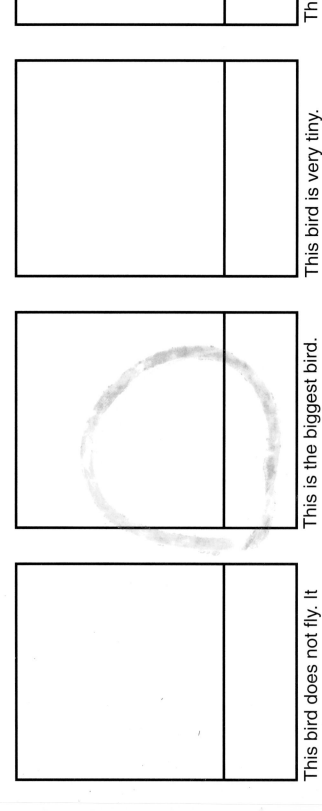

This bird does not fly. It lives at the South Pole. It is a good swimmer.

This is the biggest bird. It cannot fly. It can run very fast.

This bird is very tiny. It has a special beak for drinking nectar.

This bird likes the dark. It eats mice and other small rodents.

Bonus Box: On the back draw and color a picture of your state bird.

owl

ostrich

emperor penguin

hummingbird